Staff Talk

52 Devotions
For Church Staffs

Wil I. Jackson

CSS Publishing Company, Inc., Lima, Ohio

STAFF TALK

Copyright © 2002 by
CSS Publishing Company, Inc.
Lima, Ohio

Unless marked otherwise, scripture quotations are from the *Holy Bible, New International Version.* Copyright © 1973, 1978, 1984 International Bible Society. Used by permission of Zondervan Bible Publishers. All rights reserved.

Scripture quotations marked (TEV) are from the *Good News Bible,* in Today's English Version. Copyright © American Bible Society 1966, 1971, 1976. Used by permission.

Library of Congress Cataloging-in-Publication Data

Jackson, Wil I., 1936-
   Staff talk : 52 devotions for church staffs / Wil I. Jackson.
     p. cm.
Includes bibliographical references.
   ISBN 0-7880-1907-4 (pbk. : alk. paper)
   1. Clergy—Prayer-books and devotions—English. 2. Church officers—Prayer-books and devotions—English. I. Title.
   BV4011.6 .J33   2002
   242'.69—dc21   2002004185

For more information about CSS Publishing Company resources, visit our website at www.csspub.com or e-mail us at custserv@csspub.com or call (800) 241-4056.

ISBN 0-7880-1907-4   PRINTED IN U.S.A.

This book is dedicated to my wife Carolyn who understands a lot about management principles, especially planning, organizing, and delegating. She applies these principles well in her realm of responsibility, and the result is a well-defined home.

Thank you, Carolyn, for providing me with space and time to work on my writing projects and to, otherwise, enjoy the fruits of forty years of active ministry while pastoring local churches.

Wil I. Jackson

Table Of Contents

Foreword

Staff Talk is a book I wish I had years ago when I was appointed to my first multi-staffed church. I could have used it then and kept it in use for the next 28 years. As one might expect, most of my staff meetings began with a brief devotion and a prayer. Either I had the devotion or asked a staff member to prepare it.

I am struck by many things in Wil Jackson's *Staff Talk*. Let me mention a few. First, I am struck by the comprehensive nature of these talks. They offer a variety of themes, and the breadth of them is astonishing: from prayers for the church to prayers for the home and family. The middle parts give guidance for management principles and take the staff into the theological issues of pride, anger, sloth, and the other deadly sins. Jackson's insight reveals the various "theologies of sin management" that plague churches today, both conservative and liberal. Then Jackson offers help in making the staff aware of the great seasons of the Christian year. The resolutions he gives for a New Year are adaptable to us all regardless of whether we serve on a staff or are retired.

Second, I am struck by the accessibility of this book. I am aware that some of the topics my friend uses for these devotions are of immense importance, yet they are so understandable, so readable, so applicable. Again and again, I find my staff relations mirrored in his insights and concerns and know now that I could have done a little better job with my staff in developing our devotional life together.

In addition, everything Wil deals with is so intently practical. Never allowing issues to stay theoretical, he constantly weaves them into the warp and woof of daily experience. His stories charm. His examples teach. Most of all, he deals with human issues in wise and sane ways. This is especially true with the issues of procrastination, excuses, gluttony, lust, and others.

Third, I am struck by the depth of these devotions. Wil Jackson is a master in bringing the teachings of Jesus into everyday life. Having worked with him both in a staff relationship and as his superintendent, I am aware of his own devotion and prayer life. I also know how observant he is of the spiritual growth of others, especially in his relationship with his "saintly sexton" Onie.

The prayers that follow each talk penetrate the heart of Jesus' teachings. The entire book is well worth the prayers alone. But he gives us much more — a feast for the mind and the heart.

I am struck, and this is my final and fourth observation, by the warmth of Wil's book. He writes words of grace and mercy for us all, and especially for those of us who serve on a church staff. He offers the care of the Shepherd, lets us know of God's trust in us, and leaves us with a vision that is centered on the church's harmony with God's plan. I would place *Staff Talk* in rare company: alongside Henri Nouwen's *Bread for the Journey* and Eugene Peterson's *Living the Message*.

— Wallace H. Kirby

Author's Note: Wallace has humbled me with what he has written. From June 1968 to mid-June 1972, I was associate pastor at historic Hay Street United Methodist Church, Fayetteville, North Carolina, where Wallace was senior pastor. It was a thrilling place to be in ministry, and we have remained close and dear friends since then. For the four years I served at McMannen United Methodist Church in Durham, North Carolina, Dr. Kirby was my District Superintendent. I know no one, personally, who has a more disciplined prayer and devotional life than he. He has, at least, four books of his sermons published by CSS Publishing. The Reverend Dr. Kirby is now retired and lives in Roxboro, North Carolina.

Preface

The single most important word in the English language is "God." Words we associate with a relationship to God are also tremendously important — Jesus, Holy Spirit, cross, resurrection, faith, and so on. The most important grouping of two words is "thank you." And the most important grouping of three words is "I love you." Briefly, I want us to focus on "thank you."

It is not what we have in our pocket, or in the bank, or invested in stocks that makes us thankful. It is what we have in our hearts. Thanksgiving — real thanksgiving — is not shallow; it runs deep. Thanksgiving first focuses on God and upon our wonderful Savior. Then it hastens on to include home and family, friends and opportunities to explore, to stretch, to grow, and to become all that God intends. Obviously, there are many other themes to giving thanks: the satisfaction of work, the renewal that comes through exercise, appreciation for the beauty around us, the peace that settles in when we find contentment in our souls, and so on.

In this book we want to say, "Thanks," for good, strong churches in which to serve and for good soil in which to do our ministry. We should be thankful for church members who seek to grow in their understanding of discipleship and who stand, shoulder to shoulder, with us in the discharge of our responsibilities.

Each staff member should seek to serve with a degree of excellency. But we cannot do that, consistently, unless we have our own cups filled. We cannot show another person Christ, or Christian love, unless we have been confronted, authentically, by the living Christ.

Regular times for staff talks — for sharing the faith, for building the team, for improving communications, for establishing trust, for dreaming the future, for covenanting together, for praising God — are absolutely essential to the well-being of any multi-staffed church. Such talks should have forethought, and the principles and themes discussed should be biblically based. This author has served as youth minister, associate pastor, and senior pastor in a wide-range of church settings. He believes that what is offered in these pages is "on target" devotional material that explores concepts that will bind staff members more closely together — and to God.

Thanks be to God for the gift of himself and thanks also for the gift — the talents and abilities — of each staff member.

Wil I. Jackson

A Prayer For Our Church And For Us As Staff

O Lord, our Lord, how excellent is your name in all the earth.
We thank you for this day and for the opportunities afforded us to
serve you.

You have called us to work within the framework of this church's
life and ministry.
What each of us does is extremely important.
Yet what we do is never done independently or separately.
We are a team, and what we do in our respective staff positions is
important to the whole.

Help us to build a sense of community, to be a people of trust and
good will.
Remind us to be supporting, caring, encouraging persons — to one
another and to others.

Be with this church in its ministry and outreach.
May its members continue to grow in their understanding
of the Christian way of life and their purpose in being a part of the
whole.
They, as well as us, are called to specific ministries.
Help us to be enablers of them —
and not persons who take responsibility away from them.

Continue to move this church forward.
Increase the joy that is experienced
when we share in worship, fellowship, study, and outreach.
Make us mindful, both staff and members, to seek and to do your
perfect will.
We are called to love and to serve to the best of our abilities — and
to be faithful to you.
Nothing more and nothing less is expected.

In the strong and wonderful name of Jesus, we pray this prayer.
Amen.

The Twelve Most Desirable Characteristics Of A Church Staff Member

12. I will not fear tomorrow, knowing that God is already there (see Isaiah 43:1-3).

11. I will not attempt to remove the speck of sawdust in my brother or sister's eye without paying more careful attention to the plank in my own eye (see Matthew 7:3).

10. I will seek to be a joyful Christian, remembering that a down-in-the-mouth Christian is as much out of place as a sour pickle in a freezer of ice-cream (see Philippians 4:4).

9. I will seek to be helpful, remembering that I have been helped (see Philippians 4:13).

8. I am a dreamer who has realized enough of my dreams, thank God, to make me want to dream on (see Acts 1:17b).

7. I am a person of prayer who has seen enough answers to my prayers to make me keep praying on (see Colossians 4:2).

6. I am not a person who spends time in gossip. I do not spread rumors. I search for the truth (see Exodus 20:16 and 23:1).

5. I will find something good in every person I meet. I will look for and find a quality of value that I can affirm (see Psalm 8:4-5).
P. S. My mom said to her children,
"There's so much good in the worst of us,
And there's so much bad in the best of us
That it hardly behooves any of us
To talk about the rest of us."

4. Remembering that I am responsible for my words and actions to those who give supervision and wise counsel, I will think thoughts that are positive, seek to be productive, strive to be encouraging, and aim to be motivating as I rub shoulders with others (see Philippians 4:8-9).

3. I will remember to be a good team player on the church staff; there is no "I" in the word "team" (see 1 Corinthians 12:14-20).

2. I believe that my vocation/work is a calling whereby God has chosen me for his good purposes — and not I him (see John 15:16-17).

1. I believe one thing is needful in each new day: to seek God above all else. All other things will fall into place in good order if I will only do that first thing (see Matthew 6:33).

Part One

Theme Staff Talks

Shepherding

Psalm 23:1a: "The Lord is my shepherd...."

In forty years as a pastor, I lived in only one community where a farmer actually had a herd of sheep. Upon my encouragement the man shared some insights into the ways of sheep, enough so that I gained a greater appreciation for the biblical shepherd.

In Old Testament times there were three types of shepherds.[1] First were the nomad shepherds who owned flocks and herds, dwelt in tents, and moved from place to place to find pasture and protection for their flock. There are church staff members who roughly fit that description. They are not native to the area where the sheep (people) live but come for a season to give care (nurture) and concern (encouragement) to those who need a watchful eye. Such shepherds are "called" by God to serve in this particular pasture land and are meant to be professionals in the very best sense of that word.

Secondly, there were settled shepherds, committed to staying in their homeland for a variety of reasons. Nonetheless, their sense of commitment to the task of shepherding was just as sterling as that of the nomadic shepherd. So it is with church staff members who serve as music directors, organists, program directors, youth ministers, whatever. They and their families may never move away from the community, and so these staff persons may serve for a protracted period in their particular role. Their eagerness for their task must not wane, and their sense of calling (purpose) must not diminish.

In the third place, there were "gentlemen" sheep owners who dwelt in towns while their flocks were driven from grazing land to grazing land by their servants. By way of contrast, the "gentleman" sheep "owners" are church members who pay the bills in the local church. At times, they gain the notion that the sub-shepherds (staff) work for them. Great patience and wisdom are required of a staff member when they observe this attitude coming to the surface.

Interestingly, the "gentleman" shepherds and their families are also the sheep. Sometimes they accept responsibility (volunteer staff) that is absolutely essential to the sheepfold (the life of the

17

church). Even so, their interest can wax and wane in the activities, and even worship, that transpires in the life of the congregation.

A farmer reminded me that it is characteristic of sheep that they are easily distracted. Keeping their heads down while they nibble at the grass, they aimlessly wander from place to place — the beach, the mountains, a ball game, a golf outing, and so on. However, the expectation is that the church staff member will stay focused and that he will have a servant's heart. "Servant leadership" is what must be developed as we work together on a church staff.

Jesus is the Chief Shepherd, and it is really for him that we work, none other. Jesus knows his own sheep by name, and the practicing, growing Christian learns to obey his voice. With confidence and affection the sheep will follow him while they refuse to follow any other. Jesus met the test of supreme love for his flock by laying down his life for his sheep (read John 10:1-18).

All who have responsible positions in the life of the church — senior pastors, associates, secretaries, Sunday school teachers, mission and evangelism chairpersons, and so on — are seen as sub-shepherds of the sheep. We look to Jesus for vision, instruction, insight, and wisdom. Let us be faithful to him above all else.

Let us pray. God of olden days and God of today and all tomorrows, we thank you for sending Jesus as the Chief Shepherd of your sheep. Thank you, also, for the privilege of serving as sub-shepherds. Keep us fresh and focused for our individual tasks. Help us to understand that what we do, individually, for the flock fits together in a meaningful whole. Good shepherding is team work. Amen.

Thought for the day: Whether we are nomad shepherds or settled shepherds, we need to have a sense of calling to our particular responsibility. Being professional, in the best sense of the word, is to do our job, keeping people clearly in focus, to the best of our ability.

---

1. The idea of three types of shepherds comes from *The New Westminster Dictionary Of The Bible*, Henry Snyder Gehman, editor (Philadelphia, Pennsylvania: The Westminster Press, 1970), pp. 866-867.

Staff Talk

Psalm 23:4b: "... your rod and your staff, they comfort me."

Webster's *New Collegiate Dictionary* carries as many as six definitions for the word "staff" when used as a noun. For our devotional talk together we will limit our discussion to two main definitions: 1) a long stick carried in the hand for support in walking; a club or a cudgel; 5) the personnel who assist a director in carrying out an assigned task.

The first definition listed is the one that conjures up the image of the shepherd's staff in Psalm 23. Still, it is a bit difficult to distinguish between the rod and the staff that brought to the sheep a feeling of comfort and security. Importantly, the staff, with the crook at the upper end, was used to manage the flock, keep it together, guide it, defend it — and chastise the disobedient (see Micah 7:14a).

Charles Swindoll helps us to distinguish between the rod and the staff. The rod, for example, was a symbol of the shepherd's power. Actually, it was a hardwood club about two feet in length and was used to defend the flock against wild beasts. The head of this rod was round, usually whittled from the knot of a tree — in which the shepherd had pounded sharp bits of metal. It could do considerable damage when used to smash the head of an attacker and also could be used as a missile hurled at a dangerous animal lurking in the distance.

By contrast, the staff was his crook, bent or hooked at one end. Its utilitarian purposes included prying a sheep loose from a thicket, pushing branches aside along a narrow path, and pulling wandering sheep out of crevices into which they had fallen. The staff could also be used to beat down high grass to drive out snakes and wild beasts. Like the rod, the staff was a symbol of the shepherd's power and strength.[1]

Sheep (Christians) today can take comfort in the strength of Jesus as the Good Shepherd. None need to feel uncomfortable with the power of God in Christ Jesus. We are to find release from the tensions of the world and peace in our souls in the fact that he is able when we are not (read Ephesians 3:14-21 and especially verses 20 and 21). The Shepherd's rod and staff will protect us.

Again, church staff members are reminded that we are sub-shepherds of Jesus. If in our day we need a club or cudgel (a weapon), then let it be the Holy Bible (read Hebrews 4:12). Beyond the delineation of our various responsibilities, every staff member ought to be well grounded in Scripture. And it is by biblical principles (teachings) that the staff member must live before family, friends, co-workers, church members, and the world.

A more positive symbol is the shepherd's staff. Sheep (people) can sometimes be stubborn in their insistence on going the wrong way and need discipline (guidance) from a sub-shepherd. We are to be an enabler for those persons, not a scapegoat for their seeking an easy way out of binds and predicaments into which they have gotten themselves. Be as gentle as possible in dealing with the sheep; nonetheless, be firm. Use the staff (your authority) with assertiveness only when absolutely necessary.

When we, the church staff, are a resource for God's people, we will be a blessing. Then the sheep will say to others, "Our staff (at the church) does comfort me."

Let us pray. We thank you, O God, that we are the personnel, the staff, who are assisting this church in its reason for being: to lift Christ up that he may be glorified. Keep us faithful and strong as we continue to be "on mission" for him. Amen.

Thought for the day: The staff of sub-shepherds is to manage the flock, keep it together, guide it, defend it. When we do such, we will be a comfort and a source of encouragement and strength for each other as well as for the sheep (church members that comprise the flock).

---

1. Charles R. Swindoll, *Living Beyond The Daily Grind* (Book 1) (Dallas-London-Sydney-Singapore: Word Publishing, 1988), pp. 76-77.

Part Two

Staff Talks On The Values Of A Covenant Relationship

Covenant

Genesis 9:8-9: "Then God said ... 'I now establish my covenant with you.' "

When we serve on a church staff, either we have received a gracious invitation from the (governing) church body or we have been appointed/sent by a superintendent or a bishop. It has been believed that "the call" to serve will be mutually beneficial to all concerned. What is being formed should be referred to as a covenant relationship.

"Covenant" is a strong and beautiful word in the English language and in Christian theology. It is, for example, a much stronger word than a legal contract. With the help of a good lawyer and legal precedent, a person, generally, can find an escape hatch from a legal contract. It simply does not have the binding relationship inferred in a covenant agreement.

For the purposes of staff talk we need to distinguish between two types of covenant. The more important of the two is the one in which God consents to be a covenanting party. This makes it uniquely different from the second type of covenant in which the two or more covenanting parties are on an equality or on the same level.

In the divine covenant, God always remains on the higher level, and he, voluntarily, offers the covenant as an act of his grace. God's covenant with humankind is a gracious promise on his part, generally based on the fulfillment of certain conditions by man. In other words, a covenant contains a responsibility of mutuality (read 2 Chronicles 7:14).

Upon this covenant of our mutual responsibility is where we place focus in this devotional talk. First Corinthians 12:12, 25-26 says this: "The body [both the staff and the church] is a unit, though it is made up of many parts; and though all its parts are many, they form one body. So it is with Christ ... *so* that there should be no division in the body, but that its parts should have equal concern for each other. If one part suffers, every part suffers with it; if one part is honored, every part rejoices with it."

In partnership with one another — and with the Holy Spirit guiding our efforts — we need to covenant together that we will live by the following values in all that we think, say, and do:

1. **Trust**. "Now it is required that those who have been given a trust must prove faithful" (1 Corinthians 4:2).

2. **Learning**. "I don't mean to say I am perfect. I haven't learned all I should even yet, but I keep working toward that day when I will finally be all that Christ saved me for and wants me to be" (Philippians 3:12).

3. **Empowerment**. "Do not neglect your gift which was given you through a prophetic message when the body of elders laid their hands upon you" (1 Timothy 4:14) and "... you will receive power when the Holy Spirit comes on you ..." (Acts 1:8).

4. **Teamwork**. "Two are better than one because they have good return for their work. If one falls down, his friend can help him up. But pity the man who falls and has no one to help him up! ... A cord of three strands is not quickly broken" (Ecclesiastes 4:9-10a, 12b).

These four concepts[1] define how we will work with one another in a covenant relationship.

Let us pray. Almighty God, we thank you for the many examples of a covenant relationship in the pages of the Bible. Always you have been faithful in the covenant while, time and again, we have broken the sacred agreement. Graciously, you have taken the initiative to restore the relationship.

Cause us as a church staff, with great intentionality and purpose, to enter into a covenant relationship with you and each other. Help us to work together in mutual trust. Keep us open to new learning. Empower us to do our work and to do it to the best of our ability. Make us to be good team players. In the strong and good name of Jesus, we pray. Amen.

Thought for the day: A covenant contains a responsibility of mutuality. Each must bear his or her part of the whole.

---

1. The framework of the four concepts/values contained in a covenant relationship comes from a document prepared by the professional staff of Asbury United Methodist Church, 6612 Creedmoor Road, Raleigh, North Carolina 27613, the Reverend Marshall Old, Pastor. These values and the hyphenated meanings, enclosed in quotation marks, are the themes of the next four devotional talks in this series.

Trust

1 Corinthians 4:2: "... those who have been given a trust must prove faithful."

A Gallup poll several years ago rated members of the clergy and pharmacists highest in "honesty and ethical standards." More than two-thirds of the public gave the clergy a high approval rating, and druggists received a 65 percent positive rating. If those percentages have changed in more recent polls, let us hope that the clergy and the pharmacists are only doing better. The trust of the people we serve is at a high premium, and church staff is no exception.

"Trust within the context of the church's life and ministry means:
- mutual respect in spite of human error;
- honoring the church's vision over the individual's vision;
- sharing information and feelings without fear of intimidation, reprisal, or betrayal."

All persons, no matter how important or how powerful, do make mistakes. Henry Ford forgot to put a reverse gear in his first automobile. Thomas Edison once spent over two million dollars on an invention which did not pan out. What was your latest goof? When will the next one occur?

Some people seem to keep a black notebook on the mistakes of others. They are the people who remember all the mistakes of others but seldom recall their own. The teaching of Jesus should quickly surface: "Why do you look at the sawdust in your brother's eye and pay no attention to the plank in your own eye? ... first take the plank out of your own eye, and then you will see clearly to remove the speck from your brother's eye" (Matthew 7:3, 5).

Fellow staff members have dignity and worth all their own. Affirm them whenever possible that together we may live out the purpose to which we have been called — beyond our mistakes and failures.

George Barna, sociologist, noted that

at each successful church there was a clear understanding of God's plans to give the church a hope and a future.

26

It was not perceived to be the vision of the pastor, or of a strategic planning committee or one promoted by the denomination. It was understood as God's vision for the church. There is a huge difference between God's vision for us and the ideas we dream up on our own.[1]

The individual staff member certainly can offer input into the formulation of God's vision for the church, but he or she must trust the process and not claim it as one's own.

Let sincerity ring in our voices when we say to another staff member, "I believe in you. I recognize the possibilities that are within you, and if there is any way I can assist you, please let me know."

Finally, a trusting environment in the work place is absolutely essential. In staff meetings we ought to share, openly, our concerns, our hopes, and our fears. A trust level must be achieved where we do not feel we will be gobbled up, consumed, attacked, embarrassed, or turned on with any hint of loyalty and respect set aside. We can walk hand-in-hand without seeing eye-to-eye.

Let us pray. O God, it is amazing how much trust you put in us. As quickly as our trash basket fills and we ask you to empty its contents, you do so. You restore us quickly to dignity and worth.

Help us to be gentle with each other in the context of working together as staff. Make us determined to maintain confidentialities and to show mutual respect in spite of human error. Amen.

Thought for the day: "The only way to make a man trustworthy is to trust him; and the surest way to make him untrustworthy is to distrust him and show him your distrust." (Henry Lewis Stimson)[2]

---

1. George Barna, *User Friendly Churches* (Ventura, California: Regal Books, a Division of GL Publications), p. 87.

2. John Bartlett, *Familiar Quotations* (14th edition), Emily Morrison Beck, editor (Boston-Toronto: Little, Brown & Co., 1968), p. 893b.

Learning

Philippians 3:12: "... I haven't learned all I should even yet ..."

Materials from a high-tech corporation carried the following headline, "Intelligence Everywhere!" It is certainly the truth. The Web is leading the way in this information overload that is almost instantly available to us. Sixty-five billion smart chips are projected to be sold over the next five years. Church staffs had best be on the cutting edge of learning new methodology and ways of marketing the old, old story of Jesus and his love.

"Learning means, within the context of our covenant relationship, the following:
- patience with one another;
- willingness to take another step forward in spite of potential mistakes and setbacks;
- investing in others through our role as a coach while we accept coaching from others with an open mind and spirit ..."
— and an awareness that the biggest room in the world is the room for improvement. Someone else may have a bigger and better idea.

It all sounds self-explanatory; nonetheless, it bears repeating. Patience, for example, is something for which a lot of us pray, but never have I seen it instantly, dramatically, and forever given. It is a seed that has to be planted and slowly nurtured and watered. Patience is what we call forth when a fellow staff member is thick between the ears or when he or she has reached a high level of frustration. Patience is hanging in there and trying one more time to grasp the new thing that is being taught or introduced (see Romans 5:3-5).

Risk-taking definitely is a part of the learning process. Playing it safe certainly was not a part of Jesus' strategy. He faced toward Jerusalem knowing full well what awaited him there (see Luke 9:51b). Some called it failure to execute wisely; Christians know the rest of the story.

Sometimes in the church, and in the leadership of the staff, we put ourselves in a box. The seven deadly words risk takers dread to hear are, "We have always done it this way." Stepping out of the box, getting out of the rut means we run the risk of failure. So what? Temporary setbacks are a way to permanent improvements. We learn from past mistakes, and we hope the next undertaking will be more productive.

It is not a bad idea to think of staff members as playing coaches. We are not on the sideline calling plays. We are on the playing field every day, giving instructions, whispering encouragement, and setting an example for volunteer workers and other church members. However, we must show a willingness to be supervised as well as to supervise. We need to be motivated, cajoled, directed, held accountable. We need to be team players and assistant coaches on Jesus' strong team.

And the perfect church has yet to be built and maintained, and the perfect staff has yet to be assembled. Desiring to learn more leaves us wide open to our options and demonstrates our willingness to grow as disciples. There often is a better way of doing things in our area of responsibility.

Let us pray. Father of Jesus, we thank you that he was known as "Rabbi" to many. The great Teacher that Jesus was — and is — suggests that we have a lot to learn. Keep us open and growing as opposed to being closed and satisfied. Give us wisdom when we know that we already have knowledge. In his strong name, we pray. Amen.

Thought for the day: Temporary setbacks are a way to permanent improvements. We learn from past mistakes, and we hope the next undertaking will be more productive.

Empowerment

Acts 1:8: "... you will receive power when the Holy Spirit comes on you."

A number of years ago, a leading scientist pulled an ordinary cardboard train ticket from his pocket and said, "There is enough atomic energy in that to run an express train ten thousand miles." Then he added, "We'll tackle sand next. Sand! And in two handfuls of sand there is energy enough to supply all the basic power needs of the United States for two or three years." How many people do you suppose believed him?

Back in the 1950s a professor at Rutgers University said that there is more energy in fifteen days of sunshine than in all the world's coal deposits. Then the Reverend Harold L. Lunger made this observation, "There is more energy in fifteen men living in the spirit of Jesus Christ than in all the world's deposits of uranium!"[1]

Power! It is all around us, and, perhaps surprisingly, it is within us. Will we take the power that is ours and use it for this church's good?

"Empowerment within the context of a staff's covenant relationship means:
• sharing authority and responsibility;
• giving permission to others (delegating) with understood and mutually-agreed upon boundaries;
• listening to the perspective and opinions of others."

Other than in and through our Trinitarian God, there is no absolute power residing in this church's life and ministry. The power is shared power. There is great authority, by necessity, vested in the senior pastor who is the chief administrator — but his power is not absolute. There are governing bodies and key decision-making committees — but their power is not absolute. There is entrustment, even empowerment, to various staff members to carry out certain responsibilities — but it is not unrestrained power — freedom to do everything we please.

There is the notion that, in every day of our work, we will be true to our calling. We will give an honest accounting of our time, effort, and creativity. We will not shirk our responsibility but will seek to know and to do what is right. And when we step aside from whatever is on our plate to do, we will leave with peace and contentment that we have given our best.

Rather than being overwhelmed with the entire mantle of responsibility for a given area of the church's life and ministry, wise staff members will search for reliable and capable volunteers with whom to share their load. Such delegation to others will help lay people feel they are part of a true ministry team in doing the really important work of the church. The church is never a one-man show, except that Jesus be lifted up (read John 12:32).

Finally, there is a distinction to be made between hearing and listening. Hearing may be only a matter of gathering information. Listening is hearing with sensitivity the emotional content of what is being said. It is wise discernment. Truly listening carries with it the responsibility of making an appropriate response.

Are we willing to be empowered — to have the Holy Spirit come upon us?

Let us pray. O God, through your Holy Spirit you give us all the power we need. But do not give it to us ahead, lest we should trust in our own strength and not on your Spirit alone. Thank you, O God, for always giving enough power and strength but none to waste. Amen.

Thought for the day: There is more energy (power) in this church staff when it is in the mind and spirit of Christ than in all the world's deposits of uranium! There is always enough — but none to waste away foolishly.

---

1. Harold Lunger, "Earthquake in the Morning," *The Pulpit* magazine, April 1957.

Teamwork

Ecclesiastes 4:9, 12b: "Two are better than one because they have good return for their work ... A cord of three strands is not quickly broken."

The achievement of landing an adjunct space shuttle on the moon's surface, and the lunar walk of Neil Armstrong and Edwin Aldrin, Jr., with Michael Collins hovering above, was reported to be the greatest team effort ever put together for a single project. In one year, at its peak, the Apollo program involved 400,000 men and women at 120 universities and 20,000 industrial firms.[1]

Forging a team spirit on the church staff and letting it bubble over into work with lay volunteers is not simply a matter of assigning warm bodies to little messy jobs that, nonetheless, need to get done. Fostering a team spirit is about enabling people to minister in the name of Jesus by helping them to grow in their areas of giftedness.

Therefore, "teamwork in the context of a covenant relationship within the church staff means:
- respecting leadership and the giftedness of others;
- showing concern and compassion for team members;
- working in concert (harmony) with each other;
- accountability to others with whom we serve."

Teamwork, then, means that we do not always have to be out front, leading. The spotlight does not always have to be on us and our talents and abilities. Good leaders seek to unearth the talents and abilities of others. An aptitude test specialist concluded that most people have about eight abilities in which they are above average, and the biggest cemetery in a community is where unused talents are being buried. Church staff can do something about that waste.

For a long time, I have known that empathy is a stronger word than sympathy. Only for a short period of time have I understood, fully, that compassion is a stronger and more beautiful response than either sympathy or empathy. Sympathy says, "I'm sorry you hurt." Empathy says, "I'll hurt with you." Compassion says, "I'll stay with you 'til the hurt is gone" (Author Unknown). To show concern for a fellow staff member or for a church member until his or her hurt is gone will help weld a team spirit among us like nothing else can (see Galatians 6:2).

The Duke Blue Devils won the men's national basketball championship in 2001. Obviously, they had an abundance of talent, but their harmony (team unity) impressed me throughout the season. There was a kid (Matt Christensen) who spent far more time on the bench than he did on the playing floor; yet he epitomized for me the harmony that reigned on that team. Matt was always seen cheering his teammates on, totally involved in the game.

Here is a great quote for us to examine: "Tying two cats' tails together does not necessarily constitute unity."[2] Harmony, coming together as a whole, is absolutely essential. It means we sing in parts, not in a solo voice.

Accountability is a word that has already popped up in our staff talks on learning and empowerment — and will, likely, pop up again. It may not always be welcomed, but it is always necessary. We cannot paddle our own boats without any supervision. Let us not resist coming together, eyeball to eyeball, with our supervisor. It is a plus, not a minus, at least for most of the times.

Let us pray. Awesome God, your Son Jesus called together a team of disciples. Even so, they were, at times, in disharmony. When it happens to us as a church staff, send your Holy Spirit to unify us once more. We can accomplish so much more in unison than we can going solo. We are grateful for the opportunity of being on your team, the greatest team ever assembled. Amen.

Thought for the day: Fostering a team spirit is about enabling people to minister in the name of Jesus by helping them to grow in their areas of giftedness.

---

1. *Time* magazine, July 18, 1969.

2. H. B. London, Jr., and Stan Toler, *The Minister's Little Devotional Book* (Tulsa, Oklahoma: Honor Books, 1997), p. 74.

Part Three

Staff Talks For General Settings

Our Father's Business

Luke 2:49b: "Did you not know that I must be about my Father's business?"

Once I had a church member whose family-owned business was the oldest established business in the county. He represented the fourth generation who had operated the business. Impressive stuff, I would say. Recalling that funeral home operation made me think of the late Bishop Kenneth Goodson. Bishop Goodson, of North Carolina roots and Virginia episcopal leadership, told of his attendance at a local Rotary Club one day. The businessmen were asked to share something about their companies and how long they had been in operation. A couple of bankers, and possibly a druggist or two, seemed to claim the honor of representing the oldest companies in the city. Then came Ken Goodson's turn.

He acknowledged that prostitution is generally recognized as the oldest profession in existence, but on that day he felt inclined to claim the honor of representing the oldest business in existence. Goodson, not then a bishop, said that God's business had been around since Adam and Eve were given charge over the Garden of Eden, and if you wanted to be more specific, he added, the Christian Church was established in the Book of Acts on the day of Pentecost (see Acts 2:1-4, 38-41). Ever since that day, the Church has added to its depositors, and the number of its branches of operation keeps multiplying.

Adding to Bishop Goodson's thought, I heard just this week that 7,000 new churches (branches) open in this country every year. Sadly, there are also some that close, but, largely, it is because people die or move away from the areas where these churches were established. New life (depositors) must constantly be added to each branch to keep it growing and vital.

Unfortunately, there are some church members who view the staff as hired help. At best, church members and staff members are equal shareholders. Staff are part of the management team, and with thanksgiving in their hearts, they need to be about their Father's business.

Interestingly, this church business grew out of an only Son's foundership. But when he died, he opened up a way for all of us to be adopted sons and daughters of his Father (read Romans 8:14-17). It is because of our being heirs as God's children that we have a stake in the family-owned business.

Staff compensation is, by necessity, at different levels, but all depositors and shareholders receive the dividend of an abundant life in Christ. The pay-out on a promissory note is eternal life.

Some bumper stickers read, "I work for a Jewish carpenter." Maybe so, but he opened the bank of heaven for humankind where moth and rust cannot destroy and where bank robbers cannot break in and steal (see Matthew 6:20-21).

For staff members, the salary may not be all that great, but the benefits for them, and for any others who have accepted Christ, are out of this world.

P. S. There are no proxy ballots cast when the Board of Directors meets in heaven. We all need to be present and accounted for.

Let us pray. Father, we thank you that you do not treat us as hired help; rather you regard us as VIPs (Very Important Persons). We are grateful for the dividend of an abundant life in Christ and for owning equal shares in the family business. Amen.

Thought for the day: It is because of our being heirs as God's children that we have a stake (ownership) in the family-owned business.

Procrastination

Read 2 Corinthians 6:1-10

2 Corinthians 6:2: "... I tell you, now is the time of God's favor...."

Edward Young (1683-1765) said, "Procrastination is the thief of time."[1] And yet my high school senior class, in a moment of jest, tried to adopt as our official motto, "Never do today what you can put off until tomorrow." A human tendency is to stave off until tomorrow the unpleasant things that beg to be done today.

Staff members are not exempt from the temptation to postpone. Maybe it is a report that needs to be typed or a thank-you note that needs to be written. Perhaps it is a prayer that needs to be uttered, a word of reconciliation that needs to be spoken, a visit that needs to be made. Detailed work can be bothersome, and some people are troublesome as they interact with us.

Biting the bullet and forging ahead may be a better strategy than not addressing the situation forthrightly. The dread of something is oft times worse than following through with the actual task. And sometimes we are pleasantly surprised with the result.

Paul wrote some interesting staff advice in 2 Corinthians 6:1-2: "As God's fellow workers we urge you not to receive God's grace in vain ... now is the time of God's favor, now is the day of salvation."

Paul must have felt that even those tapped out for particular ministries in the early church could be sitting on the gift of their salvation. For him there was an urgency about responding to the gospel, and his fellow workers ought not to be performing perfunctory tasks without regard to the nurture of their own souls.

A man dreamed that he was carried to a conference of evil spirits. They were discussing the best means of destroying humans. One rose and said, "I will go to earth and tell them the Bible is a fable and not God's Word." Another said, "Persuade them that Christ was only a man." Still another said, "Let me go. I will tell them there is no God, no Savior, no heaven, no hell." "No, that will not do," they all said. "We could never make people believe those things."

Finally, one old devil, wise as a serpent, rose and said, "Let me go; I will journey to the world of people and tell them there is a God; there is a Savior; there is a heaven — and a hell, too. But I will tell them there is *no hurry!* Tomorrow will be even better than today." And he was the devil they sent to earth!

The story is fiction, but the message is fact. Paul was on target with his concern, "Now is the day of salvation." Tomorrow may be the postponement which pushes us to the brink of disaster.

There may be a multitude of things that can be put off until tomorrow. We can bluff our way and offer excuses and rationalize about a list that will not dwindle but only grows larger. But at the top of any list worth accomplishment is a steadfast relationship with Jesus as our Savior.

Paul's talk with the Corinthian staff, and with us, continues with these words: "In truthful speech and in the power of God, with weapons of righteousness in the right hand and in the left, through glory and dishonor, bad report and good report; genuine, yet regarded as impostors ... having nothing and yet possessing everything" (2 Corinthians 6:7-10). What marvelous imagery for us as we proceed into this day and into all of our tomorrows.

Let us pray. God of power who slips into our lives at the slightest hint of invitation, we have lessons to learn in overcoming our tendencies toward procrastination. Especially teach us the value of constancy in our relationship with you and with your Son Jesus. May we give a good accounting to you of our work habits, and may we be discerning in setting our priorities. May we know that today is the time of your favor. Amen.

Thought for the day: We can bluff our way and offer excuses and rationalize about a list that will not dwindle but only grows larger. But at the top of any list worth accomplishment is a steadfast relationship with Jesus as our Savior.

---

1. John Bartlett, *Familiar Quotations* (14th Edition), Emily Morrison Beck, editor (Boston-Toronto: Little, Brown & Co., 1968), p. 399a.

Knee Deep In Summer

Read 1 Kings 20:35-43; Mark 6:31

1 Kings 20:40: "While your servant was busy here and there...."

Let's be clear in the imagery that is being used: We are ankle-deep in summer within the first two weeks our children and grand-children are out of school. Knee-deep follows quickly, occurring no later than mid-July. By early to mid-August, we are chest-deep, and if we are not careful about our busyness, summer is ended, and we can find ourselves tired and without enthusiasm for the fall schedule in the church's life and ministry.

So-called "leisure time" is at a premium in this three-month period popularly known as "summer." We are well familiar with those, including us, who are "up and down" with the attendees at church on Sundays. They — and we — are up in the mountains or down at the beach. During the week, we — and they — slip away from the office and responsibilities early and manage eighteen holes of golf — or a few sets of tennis.

Parents, thinking they can catch a break from providing taxi service, find the children enrolled in Vacation Bible School — and tennis, basketball, or soccer camp in an away city. Most children plead for an afternoon at the pool — or the matinee movie — with friends who also need a ride. Medical appointments can be at a premium. Ball practices are followed by ball games. Scout and church camp are at a peak. Reading must be encouraged, and the library must be visited. Cookouts with friends and neighbors — and paybacks for sleepovers among our children and their friends — are top-of-the-list items.

Even in the summer, we remain extremely busy people, and if we are not careful, the more leisurely months will roll by us, and we will wonder where they went and why we feel so exhausted instead of refreshed and renewed.

With reference to our Old Testament lesson for this talk, Ben-hadad was king of Syria and Ahab of Israel. They were warring

41

against each other. God promised victory to Ahab, and, surprisingly, it came. The mighty Ben-hadad was brought to his knees. Ahab was merciful and allowed Ben-hadad his freedom. This greatly displeased one of Israel's prophets who judged that the Lord wanted the Syrian ruler dead. To carry his point, the prophet acted out a parable which showed the folly of not doing the tasks committed to us by God. He punctuated the tragedy of missing the will of God with these words, "And as your servant was busy here and there, he was gone...."

How many times have we allowed something — an opportunity, a deadline, a meaningful relationship — to slip through our fingers because we were too busy with other things? Busyness seems to be the curse of our day. In an age when leisure should be much more available, our schedules, nonetheless, are cram-packed. We seem to think that our busyness is a measurement of our success, our popularity, our social status — and even of our happiness.

The result may be jangled nerves, frayed tempers, and wearisome fatigue. Even in the church this is so. The effectiveness of a church is not measured by the number of cars in the parking lot from mid-morning until 9:30 at night — five nights a week. We are called to center on God and to focus on the needs of his people — not programs. Otherwise, the Church of Jesus Christ can be viewed as the church of busy bees, droning away in an endless line of meetings and activities.

We do not need to be hustling on the outer fringes and missing what is at the very core of our faith — a relationship with Christ. Jesus pleads the point with these words: "Come with me by yourselves to a quiet place and get some rest" (Mark 6:31).

Let us pray. Father God, we marvel at summer days, and we welcome a change of pace. The promise of leisure turns us on and brings out our keenest interests. But help us to see the folly when, knee-deep, we confuse leisure with more busyness.

Slow us down before we find ourselves chest-deep in summer. There has to be motivation to gear up for the activities of fall. And above all else, we should want time to bask in your presence, thus finding ourselves excited about every day of life. Amen.

Thought for the day: When we are knee-deep in summer, we ought to be involved with those things — and relationships — that bring out our keenest interest. We ought not to be mired up to our necks in busyness.

Futility — Depression — Hope

Read Lamentations 3:19-33

Ernie Pyle, war correspondent during the dark days of World War II, wrote, "My wholly, hopeless feeling about everything." Christian people do not need to hug disillusionment and despair and use them as an excuse for inertia. Our fate ought not to be determined by outer events but rather by inner attitudes. Paul expressed his faith with these words: "But thanks be to God who gives us the victory through our Lord Jesus Christ" (1 Corinthians 15:57).

We need to understand that life runs in cycles. Few persons, if any, live life on the continuum. Downswings — low moments of the soul — come to all of us. Disease, the emotional or physical loss of a loved one, a financial setback, losing our job, a blow to our self-esteem, a viewing of one's life as "a failure" — these and many others may lead us to a season of depression.

Jeremiah was known as "the weeping prophet," depressed over the sin of his people, Israel. In the third chapter of Lamentations, Jeremiah's lament runs the whole gamut of human emotions. In the beginning verse God is seen as using the rod of his wrath, not only against Jeremiah but also against Israel. God has walled in the guilty so that they cannot escape (v. 7), and even when a cry for mercy is uttered, God shuts out the prayer (v. 8). The wormwood and the gall are mentioned (v. 19), bitter and poisonous herbs that are symbolic of a person's ill treatment in life.

The man's soul cannot find peace. He has forgotten what happiness is. No longer is he expectant of any good that might come to his life. Have you ever felt that way? If you have not, there is the strong likelihood that you will.

Suddenly, there is an upswing in Jeremiah's thought pattern. There is a flash of inspiration — a dash of light in the midst of deep darkness. The man remembers, and the memory and the seed of faith bring hope. Hope returns when the writer of Lamentations remembers and writes beautifully these words: "It is of the Lord's mercy that we are not consumed because his compassions fail not. They are new every morning; great is Your faithfulness ... The Lord is my portion; therefore, I will wait for Him. The Lord is good to those whose hope is in him, to the one who seeks him" (vv. 21-25). Resignation from a biblical perspective is a great thing. It means:

- that we stop struggling against God;
- that instead of resisting him, we struggle with him;
- that instead of going against the tide, we flow with the tide;
- that instead of seeing God as our enemy, we trust him as a Parent who loves us more than any earthly parent is capable of loving;
- that we know God is fighting with us and not against us;
- that he is weeping with us instead of laughing at us.

Verse 33 says, "He does not willingly grieve or afflict the children of men." "Willingly" means "from his heart." A more accurate translation is "willfully." It is not God's intention, the desire, or will of his great heart of love that sickness and tragedy come to touch our lives.

In times of despair, people are sustained by hope, if they are sustained at all. Hope returns when we remember one thing: the Lord's unfailing love and mercy still continue, fresh as the morning — as sure as the sunrise. *This is an ample thought for any day.*

Let us pray. O Lord our God, under the shadow of your wings, may we find hope. You will support us when we are young, middle-aged, and old-aged. When our strength is of you, it is strength indeed. But when it is our own strength upon which we rely, it becomes weakness.

Help us to practice our faith and to remember that religion is not much good for anything if we have abandoned hope. Give us courage to keep on keeping on. Amen.

Thought for the day: The Lord's unfailing love and mercy still continue, fresh as the morning — as sure as the sunrise.

Christian Caregiving

Read Acts 6:1-5a

Galatians 6:2: "Carry each other's burdens...."

Caregiving is as old as the New Testament Church. In the book of Acts the name of Stephen waxes and wanes quickly. Most likely, we remember Stephen as the first Christian martyr (see Acts 7:57-60). However, we do not as easily recall that Stephen and six others were the first deacons elected to serve the body of believers (see Acts 6:5-6).

In that early church, the Twelve (Matthias having replaced Judas) did not feel that they had time to perform the more practical aspects of the daily administration of the faith community's life. So these seven deacons were assigned to general caregiving responsibilities, including the distribution of food in the soup kitchen. More specifically, they gave particular attention to the widows. This freed the elders for a more spiritual type of ministry — preaching and praying.

Every growing, vital church, sooner or later, has to face up to the fact that a system of caregiving that is not totally dependent upon the clergy has to be in place. In fact, caregiving is the responsibility of every growing Christian. Galatians 6:2 says it best: "Carry each other's burden, and in every way you will fulfill the law of Christ."

Caring words minus caring deeds may well be the most subtle form of hypocrisy that corrodes away our Christian witness in a hurting world. Caring, really caring, is active, intentional, deliberate, disciplined, loving, cheerful. It is a way of life. Caregiving is one way to put flesh and bones on an idea that Jesus himself taught and lived.

In 1995 I attended training to be a Stephen Ministry facilitator in my local church. This system of caregiving by the laity is based in St. Louis, Missouri. It is not the only way to get the laity involved in hands-on ministry to hurting and lonely people, but it is a good way. The main tenets in the Stephen Series system are:

- confidentiality between the care receiver and the caregiver;
- the ability to listen attentively and to respond to feelings;
- the willingness to submit to supervision on a regular basis;
- to relate in a non-judgmental way to the care receiver;
- prayer and the guidance of the Holy Spirit are to be constantly sought.

While at this training course, the staff encouraged the election of somebody's name we felt was unique among attendees. One name was submitted because of its length. Another person's initial and name was "I. Diehl." This person was endorsed as "the ideal Stephen minister." My table's nominee was elected. Our candidate's name was Kelso, a name from which we developed an acrostic: K — keeps confidentiality and (shows) kindness; E — embracing supervision; L — loving and loyal; S — special servant; O — obedient to his master (under the guidance of the Holy Spirit).

Who was Kelso? He was a beautiful Golden Retriever, a seeing-eye dog whose master, Dave, sat at our table. Kelso was a strong reminder of the characteristics of a good Christian caregiver.

Caregivers, including staff members, cannot fix a broken heart — but God can! Barbra Streisand sang, "People who need people are the luckiest people in the world." Some day our turn will come around to be a care receiver. Are we open to being on both the giving and receiving end of God's love and care through his people — the Church? Do not hesitate. Do not resist.

Let us pray. Healing, loving God, help us not to be resistant when others reach out to us in our time of need. And make us quick to extend the cup of cold water in Jesus' name — and to be healing agents in whatever ways possible in a hurting world. Likewise, let us, as a staff, be faithful in encouraging laity to be involved in an intentional, disciplined ministry of caring. Amen.

Thought for the day: A Christian caregiver is like Kelso: K — keeps confidentiality and (shows) kindness; E — embracing supervision; L — loving and loyal in the relationship; S — special servant; O — obedient to the Spirit's leading.

Prayer

Read Luke 11:1-4; Philippians 4:4-9

Luke 11:1: "... Lord, teach us to pray."

When I was in seminary, I had a Christian friend who was a medical student from Pakistan. One evening, Ernest sought me out while I was playing ping-pong in the graduate center. He had another med student with him and introduced him to me as a Hindu from India. Ernest said that his friend wanted me to teach him how to pray.

What would have been your response? Would you have been equal to the task, or would you have begged off from the challenge? Would you have, as I did, immediately thought of the time when one of Jesus' disciples made the same request of him?

Is it fair for anyone to inquire into the state of our prayer life? Can it be assumed that we would lead in prayer, if called upon, during the course of a staff meeting — or a committee meeting? Would we pray with a church member if we sensed that this was their need and no clergy staff were available? Would we feel comfortable sharing with a non-Christian about our personal relationship with Christ? Do we pray in our homes — with our spouse and for our children?

If the answer to all those questions is not a "yes," we need to be encouraged to do some growing. Prayer in each of those contexts is not solely the responsibility of the clergy. There is no such thing as "the professional pray-er" in those settings.

Onie was our saintly sexton in one church that I served. She could not have topped five feet with high heeled shoes, but she was a giant in her prayer life. When she prayed at staff meetings, we all knew that the angels in heaven — and God — were listening to what she had to say. At her request those angels kept watch over her bed as she slept at night. And they shook the four corners of her bed linens to awaken her in the morning. With renewal from her rest, she eagerly embraced each new day. She taught us valuable lessons about prayer and about one's personal relationship with our Heavenly Father.

For example, Onie understood that prayer was an exchange of conversation with Someone who cares for us deeply. Prayer is dialogue, not monologue. Do you remember Lily Tomlin, the comedienne? Lily Tomlin said, "Why is it when we talk to God, we're said to be praying — but when God talks to us, we're schizophrenic?" Onie Roney (yes, that was her name) not only talked to God, but she also *listened* when God talked with her.

And Onie had learned that prayer is not a labor-saving device. She did not take short-cuts in her daily practice of prayer, and she did not short-change the importance of a strong personal relationship with "sweet Jesus," as she often referred to her Savior and Friend. Dr. C. Excelle Rozelle, my religion professor in college, used to say, "When we get up from our places of prayer, we need to put shoes on our prayers." Prayer was often a task-producing endeavor for Onie. This little lady, always faithful in her labors on the church's behalf, followed holy impulses. She visited the more elderly. She prepared meals for the sick and the shut-in. She held the hand of the one who was hurt by life — and prayed for him or her openly — and in secret. She went the extra mile, inconveniencing herself when God spoke to her heart.

There are countless other lessons to be learned about the matter of praying, but none has to be mastered before we begin to form the habit. Let us speak honestly and sincerely with God as we would our most trusted friend — and as we would a loving parent. God is both!

Let us pray. Our Father in heaven, great is your name in all the earth. Forgive us for our awkwardness in speaking with you, but help us to persist until the awkwardness flees away. Then comfort us and cheer us with the warmness of your Presence.

Thank You for the great privilege of building a relationship with you through sincere, honest dialogue. Make us eager to learn more about prayer and give us the assurance that our petitions fall on listening ears and touch a caring heart. In the strong name of Jesus, we pray. Amen.

Thought for the day: Prayer is not a labor-saving device but often a task-producing effort.

Part Four

Staff Talks On
Management Principles

Planning

Proverbs 16:9: "A man's mind plans his way, but the Lord directs his steps."

Planning! Everybody plans, and if we do not, we, generally, plan to fail. Planning is usually essential to the success of any worthwhile endeavor. Things, as a rule, do not fall into place without forethought, without a plan being formulated.

In this sense of planning, we are *all* managers. We plan and manage our time. We make and execute a work plan. We outline and adjust our personal or family financial plan, as well as a financial plan that ensures the success of our endeavors at our stations of work. We plan and manage time away from our work routine for business trips and for continuing education opportunities — and if we do not, we should.

At church, we plan for worship. Perhaps, at times, we ought not to plan and control our times of corporate worship to the nth degree. The Holy Spirit ought to be moving freely among us. We plan for other programs and ministries of the church. We plan staff meetings. Good planning keeps things moving! Direction is evidenced; doing it slip-shod, or half-heartedly, will not be long tolerated.

From the beginning, God had a Big Idea which he developed into a Master Plan. He executed the plan well, and for a period of time, the world was in an ideal state. Then sin entered the world, and God had to come up with some alternate plans. The biggest alternate plan was the Plan of Salvation, and Jesus, his Son, became the key element in the execution of that plan.

In spite of man's poor choices, which breach the original plan, at least one part of the plan remains intact. Jeremiah 29:11 says this: " 'For I know the plans I have for you,' declares the Lord, 'plans to prosper you and not to harm you, plans to give you hope and a future.' " Note the verb tense is present, not past: "*declares* the Lord."

My future — your future — is not left to chance. There is a plan, a purpose that drives all of our days. There is a meaningful whole, a wonderful design, a final outcome toward which God continually moves us. History is his-story; the final outcome is in his hands.

In our work, we ought not to be content with only small plans. Our God is a great and awesome God. Think BIG! God does!

Planning as a management principle means at least three things for each staff member. One, we need a vision. We need to see in our mind's eye what we want to happen. We feel compelled to launch the vision because God's seal of approval is upon it. How do we know we have God's approval? Because we have prayed through the vision to know that it is no longer ours but his! We dream in concert with his vision, not in counterpoint!

Two, we do research. We seek out resources. We count the cost. We set down the steps necessary to carry out the plan.

Three, we persevere. A successful basketball or football coach makes a game plan, and he does not cast it aside at the first sign of adversity or miscalculation. He makes adjustments and does some fine tuning, but, generally, he perseveres in the plan.

Let us pray. O God, we are grateful that you created us with minds that can think thoughts after you. Therefore, we can share in your vision, your purpose for our lives and for this church's life. We can be a part of kingdom building — on earth as it is in heaven. Give us the will to keep at it. Amen.

Thought for the day: In our work, we ought not to be content with only small plans. Our God is a great and awesome God. Think BIG! God does!

Organizing

1 Corinthians 14:33, 40: "For God is not a God of disorder ... But everything should be done in a fitting and orderly way."

Years ago, someone told me of an overpass that had been built and then abandoned without any use, whatsoever. Out of curiosity, I drove to the site in the heart of the warehouse district and amidst a maize of railroad tracks. There it was, a concrete structure, sitting idle with absolutely nothing connected to it. The overpass bridge was up in the air with no ramps, no access, no streets, no main thoroughfare, no nothing running off it. "What a colossal waste," I thought, "a monument to poor planning and execution; expensive and time consuming but no good result from the effort."

A lot of plans in the church's life look good on paper, but they never get off the ground. They are always up in the air, never connected to anything solid. For lack of organizational skills, they fizzle and die.

The ability to organize is a key element in management principles. We manage our lives. We manage our work load. We manage the folks who work under our supervision and tutelage — and if we do not, things can get terribly messy!

For a long time now, a little placard has adorned my desk. It reads, "Just because my desk is cluttered doesn't mean my mind is two ... to ... too!" When we are distracted and when our minds are cluttered, our organizational skills are at a minimum. In an ordered, tension-free, pleasant environment our organizational skills are enhanced, and our creativity and productivity are heightened.

The organizational skills of the core of church leaders in Jerusalem were not lacking (see Acts 6:1-7). There were complaints against the Hebraic Jews by the Grecian Jews because their widows were being overlooked in the daily distribution of food. The Twelve (the staff) thought, "Better organization, better use of our time and abilities is what we need — and an expanded pool of workers won't hurt a thing!" So they had the body choose seven men (deacons) to wait on the tables while they gave more of their

55

attention to prayer and to the ministry of the Word. Some might say, "They worked *smarter*, not harder." So from the era of the early church in Jerusalem, there emerged an administrative staff and a program staff.

In today's society, some worship the quantity of work they can get out of folks and are somewhat indifferent to the quality of the output. In all that we do as a church staff, let us resolve that it be quality-driven. Is it not recorded in Scripture that we are to present (organize) "ourselves to God as ones approved, workmen who do not need to be ashamed" (2 Timothy 2:15)?

Let us pray. Creator God, you brought order out of chaos. You are an organizational genius. Who but you could keep this planet running on a daily basis, giving attention to so many details?

Please instruct us well on how to manage our time, our lives, and our work. If we do not possess organizational skills, help us to develop them. Amen.

Thought for the day: Some plans are always up in the air, never connected to anything solid. For lack of organizational skills, they fizzle and die.

Delegating

Read Matthew 10:1-8

John 15:16: "You did not choose me, but I chose you and appointed you to go and bear fruit."

While in college I worked one summer as a counselor at a church camp. That experience taught me a most valuable lesson in good management practices — learn to delegate. Let me explain.

One week my co-counselor and I had had the youngest children in the whole camp. She was pretty as a picture but could not bring hot water to a boil. The children loved her and followed her around like Mary's little lamb. I tried, unsuccessfully, to motivate them to gather dry firewood and to place it under a tarp and to put a lean-to over a table they should have lashed together from pieces of wood chopped to be of fairly equal lengths. Can you see where this is going?

The weather was bad after about the second day in camp, but by then I had given up trying to make the children act responsibly about our little "home-in-the-woods." Toward the end of their stay in camp, the director said that each group would eat at least one meal away from the central dining hall — out in the woods — regardless of the rain that had continued to come down in torrents.

What a fiasco! Our group was the last one out of the woods that night. I worked my fingers to the bone while my co-counselor kept the youngsters occupied; otherwise, the morale factor would have been at ground zero.

There are two kinds of leaders: the ones who do it all themselves and somehow think it is easier and less time-consuming to do it that way. The other kind of leader is the one who learns to delegate. Such a leader says, "I will show you how I want it done, but I will not do it for you. I will work *with you* but *not instead of you.*"

Jesus knew that his ministry and outreach had to be extended. He recognized that when his death occurred, unless he made other provisions, his important work would come to a screeching halt. So Jesus chose disciples — and still does. He appointed them (delegated them) to be, literally, his hands, his feet, and his voice so that his life of service and his preaching and teaching could continue to this very day. He said, "You are to go and bear fruit."

Interestingly, Jesus' strategy for delegating the various aspects of his ministry has worked exceedingly well — in spite of us. The Church has survived, even thrived, with workers like us. To my knowledge, Jesus never devised or implemented a Plan B. He is counting on us to produce good fruit (results) from our labors.

A further word about Jesus' use of the word *fruit* is needed. In parenthesis I used the word "results" to amplify Jesus' teaching. Even so, Bible scholar Warren W. Wiersbe warns that this is not a biblical concept. "A machine can produce results, and so can a robot, but it takes a living organism to produce fruit. It takes time and cultivation to produce fruit; a good crop does not come overnight."

Jesus is the vine, and we are delegated to be branches. "The branches do not eat the fruit; others do," Wiersbe wrote.[1] The persons who eat the fruit of our labors are strengthened in their own attempt to live the Christian life.

Delegation, then, is a way of preparing/enabling others to be his disciples and to live out his good purposes.

Let us pray. Almighty God, forgive us when we think we are the only ones who can do something — and do it right. Help us to learn the importance of delegating responsibilities. No matter our field of endeavor, we have persons who are under our influence. If they taste of the fruit of our labor, they are strengthened in their own discipleship. Amen.

Thought for the day: It takes a living organism to produce good fruit. We are that living organism. As others eat the fruit of our efforts, they are strengthened/enabled to be modern-day disciples. Learn to delegate so that they may share in Christ's ministry.

---

1. Warren W. Wiersbe, *Be Transformed* (USA - Canada - England: Victor Books, 1994), p. 43.

Coordinating

Read Nehemiah 3

Nehemiah 4:6: "So we rebuilt the wall ... for the people worked with all of their heart."

One of the most important principles of management is coordinating. The left hand simply must know what the right hand is doing — and vice versa. We cannot work solo; we must work in tandem.

Chapter 3 of Nehemiah is one of the most interesting chapters in the Old Testament. For one thing it helps determine the topography of old Jerusalem. But for the purposes of our staff talk, it stresses the importance of coordination and teamwork. About forty key men are named as participants in the reconstruction of about 45 sections of the wall surrounding the city.[1]

Someone, obviously, had to spearhead the massive operation, so we will acknowledge that Nehemiah was the chief coordinator or ramrod. Moreover, the forty men mentioned each had a crew of workers under his supervision. Interestingly, the work seems to have been done by family units as well as by certain tradesmen, professional, and regional inhabitants. Older adults, young adults, and youth, in all probability, had a part; maybe even some older children. Remarkably, for that day, we read that the workers included the daughters of Shallum (see Nehemiah 3:12).

There was opposition to rebuilding the wall, so the amount of coordination had to increase. Half the men did the work, while the other half, equipped with the weaponry of that day, were in readiness to defend the project (4:16). "Those who carried materials did their work with one hand and held a weapon in the other, and each of the builders wore his sword at his side as he worked ..." (4:17-18).

Verses 19 and 20 of chapter 4 complete our biblical insight into the matter of coordination: "The work is extensive and spread out, and we are widely separated from each other ... Whenever you hear the sound of the trumpet, join us there. Our God will fight for us."

The dedication of the workers seems obvious, and projects that grab at the heart are needed in our day. No matter what is attempted, there will likely be negative voices and factions. Only when we are well organized and coordinated, and with God's Spirit breathing life into the unfolding plan will we be able to accomplish the desired result. Our work as individual staff members may take us in different directions for days at a time, but when the trumpet sounds, we must rally together in unity and purpose. A beehive of activity without good planning and coordination must of necessity fail.

When our objectives and strategies are in God's will, he will certainly fight for us (bless us). Yoked with Christ, we find that he carries the heavy end of the responsibility himself. Our burden, and the burden of those who share with us, is made light (see Matthew 11:29).

Let us pray. O God, who changes not in the sense that your love is steadfast and sure, we thank you that you give us ideas to implement. Help us to learn the value of coordinating our plans and efforts with the plans and efforts of others. Give us the ability to motivate, so that our co-workers may work with all their hearts to bring your good purposes to pass. And if your good purposes clearly are in focus, we cannot, ultimately, fail. Amen.

Thought for the day: Only when we are well organized and coordinated, and with God's Spirit breathing life into the unfolding plan, will we be able to accomplish the desired result.

---

1. Edwin Yamauchi and Ronald Youngblood contributed to the footnotes to the book of Nehemiah, p. 888, *The Holy Bible, New International Version* (Zondervan Publishing House, 1984 edition).

Controlling

Read Exodus 18:9-11, 13-23

Exodus 18:11: "Now I know that the Lord is greater than all the gods ... he was above them."

Genesis 1:26: "Then God said, 'Let us make man in our image ... let them have dominion [control]....' "

A pilot friend flew three of us to the beach area late one afternoon to eat seafood. Flying home afterwards, he suggested that I take the controls and bring the plane in to the air base. He "talked" me through it and assured me that I was doing a good job. Later that week, I wrote Ronnie a short note and thanked him for a fine evening but expressed to him that I was never in doubt as to who was in control of that airplane as we were descending to the runway.

Good managers are always in control over their area of responsibility in the life of the church. We may "talk" others through their assignments. We may delegate as much responsibility as possible. We may coordinate the various aspects of our delegation. We may emphasize the importance of teamwork and know in our hearts that it is, nearly always, the way to do it. But a successful team has never taken the field that did not have a good coach or field general who, ultimately, called the signals.

To be in control does not mean that we have to be control-freaks. We do not need to flaunt our authority. We do not, as a general practice, pull the line taut so that others feel resentful and annoyed. Being in control should be a positive factor, not a negative one.

Being a good leader is knowing when to take up the shepherd's staff as a sign of our authority. It is to be judicious about the use of our status, our position, and our authority.

All staff persons need to learn or acquire the skill of controlling. We need to control (manage) the hours, resources, and people that are a part of our day. Control, in the proper sense of the word, is not a threat to anyone. It is a maximizer of our efforts, not a limiting factor.

Moses was a reluctant leader of the Israelite children as they escaped the oppression they had felt in Egypt. God had to show Moses that those whom he taps for a particular service he also enables. Time and again, God demonstrated to Moses that God was in control of the events of human history, not mortal men.

The verses from Exodus 18 selected for today's staff talk find Moses still growing in his understanding of leadership principles. Jethro, his father-in-law, is the chosen vessel for God's latest attempt to teach Moses new things. Jethro observes that Moses among the Israelite men is the key to the whole operation. But his control is consuming him. He needs to coordinate and to delegate. Moses does not need to involve himself with every little detail. Says Jethro, "... you will surely wear [yourself] out. For this thing is too much for you. You are not able to perform it by yourself" (Exodus 18:18). We have much to learn from this verse.

Let us pray. Almighty God, Jethro also observed that you were above all other gods. We acknowledge that you, ultimately, are in control of history accomplished — and history in the making.

And yet you have given us dominion, little spheres of influence over which we have control. Through others, teach us good lessons of management of our time and resources. Amen.

Thought for the day: Good managers are always in control over their area of responsibility in the life of the church. We may "talk" others through their assignments — but a successful team has never taken the field that did not have a good coach or field general who, ultimately, called the signals.

POD + Double C

Exodus 18:23: "If you do this and God so commands, you will be able to stand the strain, and all these people will go home satisfied."

The preceding five devotionals have been built upon five management principles that I learned many years ago. When applied well, they will work well for each member of the staff. I call them POD + Double C (Planning, Organizing, Delegating, Coordinating, and Controlling).

In the staff talk on controlling, Jethro's wisdom in instructing Moses, his son-in-law, was cited. Moses was told that he could be in control even when he delegated responsibilities. The same was true of Nehemiah as he set about the task of rebuilding the wall around Jerusalem. Both men learned how "to work *smarter*, not harder."

Jethro had first observed Moses in action. Then he evaluated, a principle on which we will need further comment. Next, Jethro conceived a plan, and then he showed Moses how to organize for action and good result. If we will appoint (delegate) officials or judges (could be a committee chairperson or a task force), we will be more effective in our work (ministry). Coordinate their efforts, Jethro said, but take care of the more difficult cases (matters) yourself. "That will make your load lighter because they will share it with you" (Exodus 18:22).

The why of implementing good management principles is also set forth in this Old Testament lesson. In verses 17 and 18 Jethro states emphatically, "You ... will only wear yourself out [if you continue doing it the way you have been doing it]. The work is too heavy for you; you cannot handle it alone." A counselor/friend said to me that he had heard that 7,000 new churches are built each year in this country. Sadly, he continued, 6,000 pastors leave the ministry each year because they feel overburdened, under-appreciated, and burned out. Other staff members, most likely, feel the same kind of stress and strain from time to time.

Study management principles, Jethro was saying. Introduce them into your area of responsibility "and you will be able to stand the strain, and all the people [benefiting] will go home satisfied" (v. 23). And you will be doubly and triply blessed if you have followed the Spirit's leading in all these matters (see v. 23).

What is our sense of priorities as we participate in the setting forth of these ideas? There are possibly four that ought to surface every day as we live before God and man:

First and foremost, everyone of us ought to give priority to nurturing a personal relationship to God in Christ (see Matthew 6:33).

Two, if we are married, our priority is to maintain a personal relationship with our spouse with whom we have a life-time covenant (see Ephesians 5:24-33).

Three, if we have children, we have an urgent responsibility to be a good parent (see Ephesians 6:4, Psalm 113:9b, and Isaiah 49:15a).

Four, there is a responsibility to our vocations (see 2 Timothy 4:5 and 1 Timothy 2:15).

Let us pray. O God, above all else, we should be led by holy impulses. Help us to learn and to apply good management principles so that we may have the stress and strain of our lives reduced. Give us a good sense of priorities. Amen.

Thought for the day: The why of implementing good management principles is set forth in Exodus 18:17-18: "You ... will only wear yourself out [if you continue doing it the way you have been doing it]. The work is too heavy for you; you cannot handle it alone."

Evaluation

Genesis 1:31: "God saw all that he had made, and it was very good."

2 Timothy 4:5: "But you, keep your head in all situations ... discharge all the duties of your ministry."

God evaluated! Shouldn't we? He orchestrated all the marvelous acts of creation in chapter 1 of Genesis; then God stood back from his handiwork and said, "It is very good!"

When the grass has been cut, when the house has been cleaned, when the sale has been finalized, when the exams have been taken, when the vacation is over, when the game has been played, do we not, as a rule, take stock and make evaluative remarks like: "Boy, I am pleased with this result," or "I wish I had studied a little bit harder," or "I wish my planning had been a little more thorough!"?

In retrospect, we are not always pleased with the result of our effort. Other times, the evaluation takes place at junctures along the way, and we amend or desist from our original plan.

How wise Paul was in his instruction to young Timothy, "Keep your head in all situations." We should not hesitate to admit that we have made a mistake, or that we are in over our heads. We should regroup or head in a new direction if and when that seems best. Do not stay with a sinking ship or with a thinly conceived idea.

Sometimes I think the crowd at the church is the last to admit that there has been a flaw in our master plan or in the execution of the program itself. Because it worked five years ago does not mean that it should be in the lineup of our church's programs this year. Ideas are for the sake of people, not for the sake of the program itself. Paul also instructed, "Discharge all the duties of your ministry." In other words, POD + Double C (Planning, Organizing, Delegating, Coordinating, and Controlling). Now I am strongly suggesting that we add evaluation to our management principles.

Evaluation not only takes place at intervals along the way and at the conclusion of a program event or emphasis, but also before the Big Idea is implemented. It is a strong biblical concept to count the cost before we begin (see Luke 14:28-32). How much will it cost in dollars? How much manpower will it take to obtain the desired results? Do we have adequate resources (parking, equipment, transportation, actual space, and so on)? Have we allowed enough time to follow through in our implementation? Is it in conflict with other items on the church's agenda?

And herein is the crux of the matter: Will this program/ministry make better disciples out of those who participate? Is there the possibility that new persons will be attracted to Christ? Will the program glorify Christ in this community and in the world?

Let us pray. Creator God, you must be constantly assessing the results of Your efforts. Keep us alert to our need to evaluate our ministries and our responsibilities. Amen.

Thought for the day: Will this program/ministry make better disciples out of those who participate? Is there the possibility that new persons will be attracted to Christ? Without a doubt, evaluation ought to be added to our menu of management principles to be digested.

Authority

Read 1 Corinthians 12:1, 4-5, 14-21, 27-28

Hebrews 13:17: "Obey your leaders and submit to their authority. They keep watch over you as men who must give an account...."

Each of us on the staff manages our time, our resources, and our area of responsibility. At times, we have oversight or supervision of other persons, at least for a season. We may or may not like that aspect of our job; nonetheless, it is our assignment to do it to the best of our ability. It is also true that others have authority over us, whether we like it or not.

Seven years out of seminary, I served at an historic old church as associate pastor. There was a saintly, elderly lady in the church, Mrs. Kirkman, who, for a number of years, had served as head communion steward. She had made it into a very prestigious position, handpicking those who served with her, and all discharging their responsibilities in preparing the elements for the Holy Supper in a most conscientious manner.

At any rate, Mrs. Kirkman made an appointment with the senior pastor, also newly assigned, and me to discuss certain matters relating to her area of work. In due time, she pointed out that there was an old chest (locked) in my study closet. Inside that chest was the old silver service (chalice and bread plate) that had been in use, let's say a hundred years ago. If the senior pastor wanted to use the chalice and bread plate on special occasions, he would notify her. If, on the other hand, I wanted to use the chalice with the youth, or other groups, in retreat settings away from the church, I was to gain permission from the senior pastor. In other words, Mrs. Kirkman was establishing her authority over this important aspect of the church's worship. With good humor, the senior pastor asked her, "And to whom are you accountable, Mrs. Kirkman? God?" Clearly, what is known as line authority had been delineated — God, Mrs. Kirkman, the senior pastor, the associate pastor — in

67

that descending order. That line authority was never challenged during my time there.

Hebrews 13:17 not only says that we should obey leaders and respect their authority over us but gives a reason for doing so: "Obey them, so that their work will be a joy, not a burden, for that would be of no advantage to you."

In other words, if we give our supervisors grief, if we gripe and complain, if we make life miserable for our co-workers, if we undermine the leader's authority, we can be sure it will double back on us. Morale will be affected throughout, and our work place will be a disaster area. God will not be glorified.

Someone has said, "It takes seven positive words to make up for the influence one negative word has on you or another person." Believe it!

In every multi-staffed church that I am personally aware of, the senior pastor is in charge of the day-by-day operations. Not only does he have spiritual oversight but also temporal oversight. The latter may not be his strong suit, but with the cooperation of each staff member, he will make a success of it.

Why does the pastor as administrator have a negative connotation for some? That is hard to figure considering that Paul, in his first letter to the church at Corinth, saw it as one of seven spiritual gifts. The gift of administration, specifically, meant that the recipient was enabled by the Holy Spirit to organize and implement plans and spiritual programs within the church (see 1 Corinthians 12:28).

Recognize/honor the one who has authority over you as a staff person. That person has 3-D powers: *Does it* — takes the initiative and makes things happen; *Delegates it* — uses the team or individual staff member to build momentum; *Dumps it* — axes it and moves the staff on to something else.

Let us pray. Almighty God, you have dominion over all that you have created. And, at our best, we are all called to be good stewards. However, in the scheme of things, in almost any setting, there is a head steward like unto Mrs. Kirkman. In the establishment of line authority, we are all held accountable. Help us to go with that flow. In the long run, it will work well for kingdom causes. Amen.

Thought for the day: "Everything is your responsibility when you're the leader — but much more so when there's a problem than when there's a victory. You share the credit and take the blame."[1]

---

1. Eileen Silvers, Bristol-Myers Squibb Co., Annual Report (2000), p. 13.

Part Five

More Staff Talks
For General Settings

Riding For The Brand
(Loyalty)

Read John 6:60-67

2 Chronicles 7:14: "If my people who are called by my name will pray and seek my face ... then I will hear from heaven and will forgive their sin and will heal their land."

A commercial for a grocery store chain caught my ear as I was riding in my car one day. The winsome voice of a cowboy was saying, "The West is not just a place but a way of life ... And a brand is more than just a set of iron initials. As an old cowboy explains to a new hand, 'Son, a man's brand is his own special mark. It says, this is mine; leave it alone.' "

Then the cowboy goes on to promote the company's long-standing reputation in the community and sows the thought that you can be loyal to this grocery store for good reason when you see its brand displayed. The commercial has this concluding statement: "We'd all be better off if more people would ride for the brand."

I could not agree more. Think about covenant relationships and team loyalties, and immediately you are into the mindset of riding for the brand. The symbolism of a couple wearing wedding rings means that other persons will know that they are taken (branded) and will respect that fact.

Jay Bilas was a Duke Blue Devil basketball player of yester-year who contributed greatly to his team's success. When he graduated from the University, he was quoted as saying that he might never again wear the uniform of his team but that the Duke blue would be forever emblazoned across his chest. In other words, he was branded for life with that identity — with that loyalty!

In that same vein, water baptism is a symbol that we belong to God through Christ. His mark is indelibly upon us, and nothing can be done to erase it. When my children were growing up, they seldom left our home and my presence without me reminding them,

73

"Remember who you are and whose you are." I was reminding them of the value of a good family name and that they are forever branded as Jacksons and as Christians.

There is community expectation that goes with recognition of "a Christian." Undoubtedly, the world — and we — would be better off if Christians would ride — with consistency — for the brand. Our "memory verse" from 2 Chronicles 7 says it well, "If my people who are called by my name...." Our representation of Christ ought to be done with loyalty and purpose — and not superficially and thinly.

The cowboy in the radio commercial also gave this advice to the young cowpoke, "... Show the boss you're making a hand. It's a sure thing he'll be there to cover your bets as long as you ride for the brand."

God is faithful to his promises. So long as we keep our part of the covenant, he covers all our bets. God forgives, heals, and restores us in the relationship far more times than we have realized. What is our part of the covenant? Our good works won't fulfill it, but the conditions set forth in 2 Chronicles 7:14 will: 1) humble ourselves; 2) pray; 3) seek his face; and 4) turn from our wicked ways (repentance).

Christianity is not a theory but a way of life. And a brand is more than just a set of iron initials. And if we as a church staff, individually and collectively, have signed on to ride for his brand, then let us protect his stock like they were our own. Some day what is his will be ours, for we are heirs and joint heirs with Christ in the kingdom of heaven (read Romans 8:14-17).

When a time of testing came in John's Gospel, chapter 6, some of the disciples (crowd) that had been following Jesus turned back (see v. 66). "You do not want to leave, too, do you?" Jesus asked the Twelve. Is it too much to ask that we ride for the brand — every day — no, every moment of our existence?

Let us pray. Father of Jesus, at times, we have one foot in the door and the other out. People who are under our influence and tutelage do not know always to whom we belong. Help us to ride for Jesus' brand consistently and help us to protect his stock as if they belong to us personally. What a privilege you have provided us to work this range (local church). Amen.

Thought for the day: The problem is not that we are not loyal but that we are not loyal enough. After all, we ride for the top outfit in the world!

What Really Matters

Read 2 Corinthians 5:14-15

2 Corinthians 5:15: "... that those who live should no longer live for themselves...."

A truly wonderful story originates out of the little town of Johnson Falls, Virginia, home of Sadie Virginia Smithson. Sadie was a nobody, socially speaking. She earned an honest but next-to-nothing existence as a seamstress. Her great ambition was to become a member of the Laurel Literary Society.

In desperation, Sadie hit upon a plan. Since no one in Johnson Falls had ever been to Europe, she reasoned that if she could make such a trip, folks would invite her to talk about her tour upon her return home. So she saved, scrimped, and skimped until she had enough money to set sail.

Unfortunately, Sadie chose the wrong time to go, for while she was there World War I broke out. She found herself trapped in Belgium. At length, an Army officer offered to drive her to Paris where she might then find transportation to Le Havre and from that port, a ship home. On the way, the driver got lost, and they found themselves crossing a battlefield. As the car came to a stop, Sadie heard a wounded soldier cry out, "Water, for God's sake, water!"

Responding with great urgency, Sadie found water and gave it to the thirsting soldier. Throughout the long night, she went from one soldier to another, giving them water, binding up wounds with bandages made from her skirt, scribbling last messages for dying men who would never see their loved ones again in this life. When dawn broke, an ambulance drove up, and a young medical officer shouted to her, "Who are you, and what in thunder are you doing out here on this battlefield?"

Sadie replied, "I am Sadie Virginia Smithson, and I have been holding back hell all night." Later, on shipboard bound for home, Sadie recounted her incredible story to a fellow passenger who remarked, "Well, the Laurel Society will surely be glad enough now to have you belong." Sadie thought about that possibility for only a moment before saying, "But you don't understand. I've been face-to-face with war and death and hell and God. I've been born again. Do you reckon any of those little things matter now?"

Her new friend asked, "What does matter?" "Nothing," Sadie answered, "nothing but God and love and doing things for folks."

Every time I hear that story retold it makes my spine tingle. Sadie Virginia Smithson of Johnson Falls, Virginia, learned some of the most valuable lessons of life in a hellish place, and she was never the same afterwards. There are few words in the vocabulary of Christianity that have greater meaning than "serve," "service," or "servant." They all translate into Sadie's enlargement on love — "doing things for folks," or giving them a cup of cold water in the name of Jesus (see Mark 9:41) — or binding up the wounds of those hurt by the crush of life — or listening compassionately.

Learning what matters in life is a discovery process. We meander through the accumulation of things, and we desire financial security. Men pursue what the world has told them is manly. Youth experiment and repeat the mistakes of past generations, thinking they have all the answers when, in fact, they do not. Women seek a more far-reaching understanding of their femininity. We all come up short.

All of us need to learn, like Sadie, what is really important in life. What is really important is God (and Jesus) and love and doing things for folks.

Let us pray. Awesome God, we thank you that Jesus visited the battlefields of earth. Consequently, he has held back hell for eternity! Reiterate to us as a church staff the need to pour out our lives in love and service to others. Amen.

Thought for the day: "Nothing (matters) but God and love and doing things for folks." — Sadie Virginia Smithson

Heritage

Read Joshua 24:13-16

Psalm 61:5: "... You have given me the heritage of those who fear your name."

Chapter 24 of Joshua deals not with the end of Joshua's ministry and leadership but with the apex of his career. Israel had overrun the center and perhaps the south of Palestine. Some of the people conquered had been absorbed into Israel's tribal alliance. Now anyone who knows anything at all about the history of Israel knows that they have always been a covenant people, chosen by God and promised his blessings for as long as they remain faithful.

For the reasons mentioned, Joshua saw the need to extend the covenant to people not previously under it. Joshua lay the matter squarely before all those under his authority. A choice must be made: the Lord Jehovah God — or — the gods which your fathers served in Egypt and Mesopotamia — or — the gods of the Ammonites in the land in which you are now dwelling.

The covenant, or the pact between them and God, was a free and moral act. As staff members, we, too, are engaged in that same covenant relationship. Every day, we seek to put away all other gods and to serve the Lord only. It is our heritage, and it is our conscious choice.

Joshua said to the people of his day, "Thus the Lord God of Israel says, 'I have given you a land for which you did not labor and cities which you did not build, and you dwell in them; you eat of the vineyards and olive groves which you did not plant.' "

As a kind of paraphrase to that, a lot of churches could say to the church staff and to a goodly number of the members, "The people who were here before you have given you a church home for which you did not labor, a sanctuary you did not build, and you worship here. You attend Sunday school for your nurture and growth. Look at your heritage. Consider the days and years, the dreams and the effort that have brought this church to the point that it is at today."

I read about a little country church that closed its doors a number of years ago. One of the members said, "We'd like to keep it as a shrine." Within us is the urge to say, "Churches should not be shrines to preserve what once was; rather churches should be alive, vital, body-filled places where people come to worship and praise the living God."

Today we are reminded of the rich heritage of this church. Our past is worth celebrating, but it does not matter from whence we have come if we do not know where we are going and to Whom we belong. Only with God as the Chief Engineer can we build the bridge from today to all of our tomorrows. What is at stake? Eternity for our children and grandchildren, for our spouses, for our friends and neighbors, for those presently in this household of faith — and for ourselves.

There is a choice set before us: "Choose this day whom you will serve, but as for me and my house we will serve the Lord." To choose the Lord — to serve him with sincerity and with gladness — is a wise choice — past, present, or future.

Let us pray. Jehovah God, we thank you that, graciously, you have invited us into a covenant relationship. We thank you for our rich heritage in the faith of our fathers and mothers.

All the programs and ministries that we have stewardship over in the life of this church ought to make possible the extension of the covenant to others not previously under it. We ought to give persons, with intentionality, the opportunity to choose you — to respond freely to the life-changing gospel that comes through Christ Jesus. Amen.

Thought for the day: Our past is worth celebrating, but it does not matter from whence we have come if we do not know where we are going. And we have a moral imperative to extend the covenant to people not previously under it.

Excuses, Excuses, Excuses

Suggestion: The leader for this staff talk may wish to use symbols for each of the three excuses cited. For example, a filled calendar for business interests; a golf club for anything which consumes us; and a wedding ring or family photo for the demands of home life.

Read Luke 14:15-24

Luke 14:18: "But they all alike began to make excuses."

Jesus told a parable about a man who gave a great banquet. The invitation list was quite long. When the time of the event drew near, the invited guests all began to make excuses. One had bought a field and had to go and inspect his real estate. Another had bought some new oxen and was intent on trying them out. Yet another had just married and did not want to be taken away from his honeymoon.

Staff members are not unlike other people. We have been chosen for specialized labor in God's vineyard — and in our day we often offer excuses, one after the other, for not doing certain things. At times, it seems possible that we are in danger of missing the Kingdom of God, and, for certain, we are missing much of the joy of our salvation. A banquet equals celebration, laughter, joy, gaiety, and exchange of conversation with the host. In short, a banquet is a gala occasion for invitees to enter into the Lord's presence. Our excuses are what they are — excuses — nothing else! They are flimsy indeed in the light of such a gracious invitation.

Let this *filled calendar* represent the labor of our hands and minds. Sometimes we become so obsessed with our work and the tasks that have to be performed and the meetings that we are asked to attend that we forget we have a soul that needs to be fed at the Lord's banquet table. An unbalanced life means something is lacking. Too often, it is a carefully maintained relationship with Jesus the Christ.

The late Dr. William Barclay, a Bible scholar from Scotland, said the second excuse offered in Jesus' story is that of a man whose passion is novelty. He has a new possession and for the moment he is preoccupied with it. So consumed with his newfound interest is the person that for awhile he puts everything else out of his mind — and heart.

I have here a *golf club* as a symbol of something which can engulf us, that can override our sense of priorities. Some people want to play golf or read, or see a video or surf the Internet, or play computer games — or go somewhere — all the time. They forget that a human's basic need is for God. We should not overlook God in our attention to new enthusiasms, the latest fad, new activities, new friendships, new loves — or old patterns — which distract our view of life and blind us to eternity.

The third excuse offered in Jesus' parable might be identified as the demands of home life. There is a paradox about our homes. They are the most important place in our lives, and rightly so. Our love for family should be solidly in place. We spend, or should spend, more time at home than any place else. So, in one sense of the word, it is true to say that no claim can come above this one.

Still it is possible to take an entirely selfish view of home and family. We can regard home as existing for nothing but our own pleasure and convenience. We can make home a place that is a castle, or fortress, that keeps the world and the needs of others out in the cold. I have here a *family photo* as a symbol of love and the family — but also as a symbol for some of our excuses when summoned by God for no other reason than to be in his presence and to celebrate his joy.

In summary, all the excuses the invited guests gave for not attending the banquet were in and of themselves good reasons. But one of the great dangers of life is to let the good interfere with the very best. The best is found in steadfast devotion to the Lord of all life.

Let us pray. O God, you truly want us to find a more abundant life in Christ. Forgive the excuses we offer in the postponement of that

great discovery. Bring us to a time in life when nothing can interfere or distract us from the very best that you have to offer. Amen.

Thought for the day: A busy schedule, a passion for recreation or
for a new interest, even home life can distract us from the pure joy
of God's presence.

If You Had It In The Church, Would You Lose It?

Read Revelation 3:14-22

Revelation 3:15: "I know your deeds, that you are neither cold nor hot ... so, because you are lukewarm — I am about to spit you out of my mouth."

A senior pastor, serving in an urban setting, made it his practice to change the bulletin board on the front lawn of the church grounds every Monday morning. A lot of passerbys were attracted to the one-line messages, such as:
- "Don't expect a million dollar answer to a single ten-cent prayer."
- "A little kindness from person-to-person is better than a vast love for all of mankind."
- "Religion is not cake for special occasions; it is bread for daily use."

One day while this pastor was out following his little routine, a seedy-looking man came whistling across the street toward him. The two men exchanged brief, polite greetings. Then the stranger asked, "You go to church here, do you?" The pastor replied, "Yes, I do. Do you?" To which the stranger gave a haunting reply as he turned and walked away, "Nope! If you had it in the church, you'd probably lose it!"

Before we discuss what the man might have been thinking, let us think positively about what "our" church has meant in the lives of persons in this community over the years of our existence. People have come here to worship and praise God; to find escape from the tensions and pressures of the everyday world; to seek forgiveness and reconciliation with God and neighbor (perhaps spouse) when we know there has been a severance or a fracture in the relationship; to find wholeness following the shattering of hopes and

83

dreams; to experience wellness when a sick feeling engulfs us after we have cheapened life; to celebrate when things have gone well, when our plate is full, when our hearts know love and when our souls are content and radiate joy and purpose.

Untold numbers have wept silently in this place of public worship; others have made important, life-changing decisions here. Couples have been joined in holy wedlock at this altar. Parents have brought infant children here for holy baptism — or for dedication. They have watched with approval and satisfaction when their children have been nurtured in our Sunday school and, have come to a point of making a decision to be a disciple of Jesus — for a lifetime. Families have held memorial services here for their loved ones who have died. For some, too timid to enter and to seek fully the ministry and life of this body of believers, it, nonetheless, has been the hem of the Master's garment, bringing comfort and hope each time they have passed on the street. In sum, people have changed dramatically the course of their lives because of the ministry and guidance of this congregation who seek to be faithful to Christ and obedient to his Holy Spirit.

But what happens if we become complacent, or if we are encrusted with moldy traditions and patterns of doing things? Or if we lose enthusiasm and direction and if we have no genuine outreach? Or if we let old family and individual hurts get in the way, or if we lose the joy of our salvation and find worship an empty routine, even an exercise in futility? Or if the church loses its vision, and division erupts?

Is it possible that we in the church (staff, members, and other participants) could have something precious and good, only to have it slip through our fingers? Could God become so distant for us that he is mostly un-reality?

What is it that we are communicating to the community of which we are a part? Is it that we have something that the people "out there" need to latch onto — or that they need to avoid at all costs? Are we magnets to Christ — or repellants?

Let us pray. Holy God, we do not wish to be like the Laodiceans — prideful about their business enterprises while their souls were bare before your presence. In their church life, they were neither cold nor hot, only lukewarm.

Send your Spirit to re-awaken us, to energize us, to direct us. Whatever is good in the life of this church cause us to build upon it and to multiply it — always and only to the glory of your Son Jesus Christ. In His name we pray. Amen.

Thought for the day: The church is in the life-changing business. How can we as church staff enhance the ministry and guidance of this body of believers?

It Takes A Lot Of Slow To Grow

Read Ephesians 4:11-16

Ephesians 4:14-15: "Then we will no longer be infants, tossed back and forth by the waves ... Instead ... we will in all things grow up...."

A church member, ninety-plus years of age, confessed to me that she had been dipping snuff since she was in her early teens. While watching a television evangelist, she had gotten under conviction that she ought to give up the habit. For the first time, she said, she was realizing that her body was the temple for the Holy Spirit's indwelling (see 1 Corinthians 6:19-20). "Remarkable!" I thought. "It does take a lot of slow to grow!" We, no matter our chronological age, never reach a stopping place in our growth into the fullness of Christ (see Ephesians 4:13).

We need to look at our lives. Where were the growth points? What were the triggers? When did stagnation occur? Are we satisfied with where we are in our Christian growth and development? What are the evidences of a life-changing gospel at work in us? Maybe we should stand perfectly still, and with chalk in hand, reach down and draw a circle around ourselves. Within that circle is the possibility of a new spurt of growth.

Let's go at it from another perspective. All of life seems geared to a fast pace and convenience. Short-order restaurants, drive-in banks, ready cash, instant credit, one-hour cleaners, minute-marts, and in Florida fifteen-minute worship services for the convenience of Sunday worshipers. There are even funeral homes with drive-in windows. People can drive up, sign the book, and pay their respects to the deceased and move on, without exiting their cars.

One wonders if we will ever get to heaven. Chances are, if we do, we will be in such a hurry that we will run right through the pearly gates — and on out the back door. We are a people plagued by the clock and a time schedule that must be kept. A poem describes well our hurry-scurry existence:

There go the grownups, To the office, to the store,
Subway rush, traffic crush, Hurry-scurry, worry, flurry.
No wonder grownups can't grow up anymore;
It takes a lot of slow to grow![1]

Someone has said that it takes the average husband and wife seven to ten years to learn each other's ways and to adjust accordingly. Spin the developing thoughts around. It does take a lot of slow to grow — in our marriages, in our relationships with our children, in the arena of developing friendships — and in relationship to Christ Jesus.

Conversion is not just an initial act, though a conscious choice to turn one's life toward Christ and to commit one's self to him is absolutely imperative. True conversion is a daily walking, sometimes painfully slowly, in a new direction — toward Christ, not away from him. There are always pockets of resistance. And there is a falling away from grace as well as a growing in grace. There are denials and betrayals and periods of sluggishness. And there are times of resoluteness, great effort, and tremendous advancement.

Think about it long and hard. It does take a lot of slow to grow, does it not?

Let us pray. Creator and Sustainer God, bring the promise of our re-creation plainly into view and then into reality. In spite of the detours and the side roads that we insist on taking, lead us to the abundant life in our day.

Through Christ, confront our lives, challenge our decisions, and carefully sift through our value systems. Change us by your power and your grace, no matter how painfully slow the process may be. In his strong name, we ask it. Amen.

Thought for the day: True conversion is a daily walking, sometimes painfully slowly, in a new direction — toward Christ, not away from him.

---

1. Eve Merriman, "On City Streets."

Part Six

Staff Talks On
The Seven Deadly Sins

PEAS Can Grow Larger

Hebrews 12:1: "... let us lay aside every weight and the sin which so easily ensnares us...."

Sometime in the sixth century, Saint Gregory the Great identified the human weaknesses we have come to know as the seven deadly sins: pride, envy, anger, slothfulness, covetousness, gluttony, and lust. Today we tend to downplay the naming of such sins, for they strike too close to where we are standing. We have been told, often, that God loves us and accepts us just as we are; so why do we need to change our attitudes and behaviors? Does not Jesus justify us before the throne of God's grace? He pleads our case convincingly, not because we have merit but because he is, so solidly, in God's good favor for seeking our redemption upon the cross.

Being ever so grateful for Jesus pouring out his very life, Christians should be fully motivated to prune away the sins that grip us so tightly. We ought to be growing in our capacity to love all the peoples of the earth. Christian love knows no barriers and withholds itself from no one. Christian love does not seek its own way, for it is God's way that we want to pursue. God's way challenges us to feed the hungry, to clothe the naked, to welcome the stranger, to visit and heal the sick, and to lift up the fallen.

Above all else, this personal and corporate response to Jesus' redeeming action of love calls us to a life of service and love. We want to draw every human being into the reality of God's love, pursuing them, wooing them, winning them. So, individually, that means we need to change and grow and have the pride, envy, anger, and so on obliterated from our lives. Grace saves us, but grace also triggers a life transformation from the sin that so easily entangles us (see Hebrews 12:1).

Why are they called the seven deadly sins? Thomas Aquinas suggested that they are deadly because they can lead us to even worse offenses. Basically, these identified sins are virtues carried to sickening extremes. We are to love self — but we are to love others equally. We must eat — but we can become gluttons. It is okay to admire something that someone else possesses — but if our admiration, our desire for that possession, becomes obsessive, we call it envy or jealousy or covetousness.

For each of the next seven weeks, our staff talks will center on these attitudes and behaviors. Which ones have their claws in us and need attention? We may be surprised upon closer examination.

Dr. Joseph B. Mullin, while he was Senior Pastor at First Presbyterian Church in Greensboro, North Carolina, provided his preaching audience with a scheme whereby Christians can easily identify these seven deadly sins. All we have to do is to remember one sentence that contains four words: PEAS Can Grow Larger. Use the four letters of PEAS as an acrostic — and then use the first letter of each of the last three words. Here is the result: PEAS = Pride, Envy, Anger, Slothfulness; Can Grow Larger = Covetousness, Gluttony, Lust.

Let the sentence sink in, and may our minds and hearts be in earnest in seeking their eradication from our lives.

Let us pray. O God, the Author of the plan for our salvation, give us inner resolve to lay aside the sin which so easily ensnares us. Let nothing have a death grip on us. We thank you that our relationship to Jesus and the power of his Spirit can keep us freed up for the benefits of everlasting life. Amen.

Thought for the Day: "PEAS Can Grow Larger."
— Dr. Joseph B. Mullin

Pride

Read: Luke 18:9-14

Proverbs 16:18: "Pride goes before destruction, and a haughty spirit before a fall."

An architect friend complains that many of his clients engage him to design a house for them, only to let him speedily discover that they have already designed it for themselves. What they really want him to do is to sanction their forethought and give them the satisfaction of seeing him draw on paper what they have fully conceived in their own minds.

In very much the same way, we often go to God, the Master Architect, with a plan for our lives. We ask for wisdom and guidance, as did Solomon, but we have already determined how we will build our future and how we will steer our course. Such self-determination also affects the course of those under our influence: family, friends, co-workers, and in this instance of church staff, church members of varying ages, depending upon our role. Plainly and simply, sometimes it is not God's way that we are really seeking; rather it is his approval of our way. That is the very nature of pride — that we know better than God what is in our best interest and in the best interest of those under our influence. Pride is a matter of usurping God's rightful place in our lives.

Actually, the English word "pride" has several shades of meaning. For example, it is okay to take pride in the way we look, but when how we look becomes an obsession, our pride becomes vanity, a turn-off to many who know us. Or, some people are proud when they have a stick-to-it-ness which allows them to overcome the odds and to master a particular goal. But when pride has puffed itself up within them, they are heading for a fall.

Repeatedly, the Bible emphasizes that pride has its root in self-centeredness. In this aspect, it is not only the ugliest of the seven deadly sins, it is also the parent that gives birth to every other sin. And pride is the one sin from which none of us can claim complete freedom. We may win mastery over envy, anger, slothfulness, covetousness, gluttony, and lust, but who among us can claim that we do not, at times, promote self above all other considerations?

Look closely at the Pharisee described in the recommended passage from Luke. The unfolding story of the two men praying in the temple says that the Pharisee "stood and prayed thus with himself." No, he did not make graven images out of stone and precious metals. But he did have our tendency to fashion God in his own image.

Pharisaism as a class is as non-existent as the dodo bird, but Pharisaism as a spirit survives to this very day. The difference: the New Testament Pharisee was thankful that he was not like other people; today's Pharisee is thankful that he is like his peers: stubborn, prideful, self-sufficient, unchanging in ideas and behavior. Pride is the tendency to put the great inflated *me* at the center of our world, a place that should be reserved only for God.

Have you ever heard of a "hamster rat"? When a hamster rat gets a grip, rather than yield, it will allow itself to be beaten to pieces with a stick. If it seizes a person's hand, it must be killed before it will relinquish its hold.

How like this hamster rat is our own proud, unyielding, sinful self! Our selfish spirit will cling to and suck the life out of any other entity that gets in its way. Are there traces of pride taken to an extreme in our work as a church staff? As an individual staff member? As a human being living in the home and in the world?

Let us pray. Merciful God, forgive us when we seek to place ourselves at the center of our home life or church life. Prick us to awareness when we are too puffed up or when we think of ourselves more highly than we ought to think. Amen.

Thought for the day: Pride is the tendency to put the great inflated *me* at the center of life, a place that should be reserved for God only.

Envy

Read John 3:22-30

1 Corinthians 13:4: "... (love) is kind; it does not envy...."

Envy knocks at every person's door. It is when we answer the knock and allow envy to come into our minds and spirits for any extension beyond the briefest of moments that damage ensues. Envy is an intrusive force, and when we give this vermin permission to linger, it consumes us — and the times of our discontent quickly multiply.

Things can look so beautiful when they are in the possession of another. Talents or abilities can be so attractive when we see them resident in someone other than ourselves. We wish like the dickens it could be us. Envy springs up because we are not content to be what God made us, uniquely different from all others that spring from God's creative genius.

Even pastors, other staff members and church members have been envious — jealous — of another church's physical properties, staff, financial resources, and so on. For shame! God does not call us to be duplicates of some other church's youth or music ministries, of their missions program, whatever! He calls each church and each church staff not to be successful but to be faithful and obedient to the Spirit's leading.

Knowing that envy lurks inside us, there are at least four things that we can do that are constructive:

1. We can learn to accept ourselves and our abilities. James Dillet Freeman penned these words in a published meditation over twenty years ago:

   God, I give thanks for many things,
   But most for being me —
   As well as I can tell,
   Myself is what I'm meant to be.

95

I might have been much more,
Perhaps a wise man or a saint,
But I'll not fret with vain regret —
I can't be what I ain't.

I might have been much more, no doubt,
But I am all I've got,
So I'll give thanks for what I am
And not for what I'm not!...[1]

If only we would try to do our best, if only we would develop the full potential that is within us, there would be no
drive to be like someone else. God has given to each of us
certain gifts and graces, and we should be satisfied in developing those.

2. We need to foster a good self-image. The only real way to do
    that is to see others as persons of worth and dignity, the same
    as ourselves. We must be a plus person in relationship to an-
    other plus person. Neither of us can be a minus. God's chil-
    dren are fantastically wonderful human beings.

3. Think more of the cause, the movement, the work than the
    status of the individual or the institution involved. Plainly and
    simply, glorify Christ in your individual life and in the life of
    this local church.
        Remember that John the Baptist was at the crest of his
    career when Jesus began his public ministry. Immediately,
    John's influence began to wane. His best followers left him
    and went with Jesus. What was John's response? "He must
    become greater; I must become less" (John 3:30). John was
    more focused on what was at stake than he was in attracting
    attention to himself. If we put Christ's cause first, then we will
    keep perspective and avoid pride and envy spoiling our good
    and best intentions.

4. The first three things written for our staff talk are suggestions;
    the fourth thing is a rule. Someone saw a sign on a great man's

wall which read, "Remember Rule #4!" He asked the great man what Rule #4 was, and the man answered: "Don't take yourself too seriously." The first man then asked, "What are the other three rules?" This time the great man replied, "There aren't any other rules."

If we don't take ourselves too seriously, then maybe we can learn to laugh at ourselves and to accept our limitations, as well as affirming our peculiar talents and abilities. Maybe we can learn to appreciate others rather than envying them.

Let us pray. O God, unburden us from our shadow thoughts of pride, envy, and jealousy. We are thankful that you created us uniquely to be ourselves, no one else. Amen.

Thought for the day: We will remember Rule #4, that we are not to take ourselves too seriously — and that we are plus persons in relationship to other plus persons. No minuses are allowed.

---

1. James Dillet Freeman, *Daily Word*, November 1981.

Anger

Read Ephesians 4:26-27, 29-32; Matthew 5:21-22, 24

Ephesians 4:26: "In your anger do not sin...."

Anger is an honest emotion. It bubbles up in response to what we see, hear, and otherwise experience. It is not the feeling itself which is a problem; it is the way we *express* the reaction that is either healthy or unhealthy. The Apostle Paul recognized the accuracy of that statement when he wrote to Christians at Ephesus, "In your anger do not sin...." Sin is that which alienates, fractures, deteriorates, or severs a relationship with God and/or with our spouse, child, friend, co-worker, and so on.

Maybe it will be helpful if we learn to identify *three types of anger.*

One, there is *destructive anger* which says, "I will carve you up into little pieces if you make me mad. I will destroy you. What I feel is all that matters; you are a nobody. I don't care how badly I hurt you with my words and actions." Fortunately, most of us who respond with this kind of hostility get over it very quickly. Unfortunately, a whole lot of damage can be done in a short period of time.

Two, there is *repressed anger*, anger which is pushed down, bottled up, contained. We sometimes refer to this as depression — anger which is turned inward on the pathetic self. Depression can be even more dangerous than overt, inappropriate expressions of anger. Such repression poisons our insides. Sooner or later, the lid must be let off and what comes out can be unhealthy indeed.

Three, there is *constructive anger.* Such anger sees a wrong or an injustice and seeks to correct it. In its expression such anger focuses on issues, not on persons. Constructive anger seeks to rebuild a relationship and to restore good communication; it does not seek to destroy, undermine, or undercut others.

Take note of this enlargement on Paul's teaching about anger in Ephesians 4: "... Do not let the sun go down on your anger" (v. 26). After we recognize our anger, then we should seek to express it appropriately and to let it cool as quickly as possible.

We need to rate our anger. Is the real cause of our anger worth being this upset? Was the provocation really directed at *me*? Maybe the more appropriate question would be: "Why did she do that stupid thing in the first place? I'm certainly not to blame for her problems and feelings, and I will not let her behavior become a personal liability to me and to my happiness." Someone has said, "The size of a person can be measured by the size of the thing that makes him or her angry."

Next, we need to choose a realistic course. Sometimes the best thing we can do about a situation where sparks have been flying is to do nothing — or to at least let the matter cool. Oft times, the circumstances will turn out to be an unimportant, momentary shudder which is quickly forgotten.

However, we must not confuse this suggestion with resentment that continues to smolder. There are some issues that will not go away. Reconciliation must be sought. Confrontation must be initiated by someone — when the timing is right. This is biblical. Jesus said, "... whoever is angry with his brother without a cause shall be in danger of the judgment." Then he continued with these words, "Therefore, if you bring your gift to the altar, and there remember that your brother has something against you, leave your gift there before the altar, and go your way. First be reconciled to your brother, and then come and offer your gift" (Matthew 5:22, 24).

No matter what other ministry we have been called to within the Body of Christ, each staff member is called to a ministry of reconciliation. Paul penned with accuracy and beauty these words: "Now all things are of God, who has reconciled us to himself through Jesus Christ, and has given us the ministry of reconciliation ... Therefore, we are ambassadors for Christ, as though God were pleading through us: we implore you on Christ's behalf, be reconciled to God" (2 Corinthians 5:18, 20).

Let us pray. Most holy God, there have been times when you have been angry with us — and rightly so. Yet you are quick to forgive and to restore.

Help us to understand our call to be peacemakers and to be involved in a ministry of reconciliation. Give us the wisdom to know that we should not allow the sun to go down on our own anger. We will not have peace in our souls as long as there is unresolved anger within us. Amen.

Thought for the day: "The size of a person can be measured by the size of the thing that makes him or her angry." (Anonymous)

Slothfulness

Read 2 Thessalonians 3:6-13

Proverbs 12:27: "The lazy man does not roast his game...."

   Surely out of the classical seven deadly sins we are on our best behavior with slothfulness! As described in Proverbs, a sloth is too lazy to prepare his food properly. That is not us! As professional church workers, if anything, we are workaholics.
   But hold on! Maybe we need a closer look. Being inclined toward slothfulness means more than being too lazy to work. In the Middle Ages, the word used to lay bare the sin of sloth was "acedia." The word is from the Greek (*akedia*), and the last time I looked it was still in the English dictionary. The second definition listed after "sloth — one of the seven deadly sins" — is "spiritual torpor and apathy." Acedia, then, is the devitalizing of our energies — physical, mental, or spiritual, or collectively — which is the price we pay for drifting into apathy and indolence. If we adopt an "I can't be bothered attitude," before long our attitude will be "I couldn't care less." This attitude can be manifested at the physical level in the matter of exercise or in the execution of good work habits; at the mental level in the reading of good books and in the expanding of our minds in serious reflection; at the spiritual level in the neglect of spiritual nurture through prayer, Bible study, and private and public worship. Acedia — torpor — leading to apathy is a deadly sin, and acedia must be counteracted with good balance in our lives (see Luke 2:52).
   There is one other definition at which we need to look. "Quagmire" means "wet, boggy ground, yielding under the feet." To be standing in a quagmire means that we find ourselves in a difficult and dangerous position. We do not understand how we got ourselves into this mess, but it happened. Maybe we got too addicted to playing computer games — while at work. Maybe we got too used to sleeping a little beyond the alarm clock — and coming in just a little late to work. Perhaps we became too accustomed to

telling the little white lie to get us out of the moment of confrontation by our supervisor. Maybe we took too many shortcuts from good work habits. Maybe we just did not give an honest accounting to God or man. Maybe we are not who we want to be in relationship to who God is. Now the quagmire, the accumulation of mud and slime, is catching up to us. That torpor is closely akin to the sin of slothfulness.

Could it be that Jesus directed us to pray, "Give us this day our daily bread ..." as a safeguard against the illusion of independence and self-sufficiency? He wanted us to be reminded that even in the midst of good paying jobs and sophisticated technology, we live in the vast sea of God's nature to give good gifts. We are all debtors to God's generosity. No matter how much we give in hours of work or in dollars and cents, we can never pay, or repay, what God has given to us. And it is precisely because we cannot really pay that we need to pray instead, "Give us — not sell us — this day our daily bread."

Our inconsistent gratitude, our inability to keep our lives disciplined and focused, really is rooted in the sin of slothfulness. Too many persons simply remain shallow, naïve, and indifferent in their growth as Christians. They stay forever spiritually flabby — and unchanged.

As staff members, let us keep a careful eye out for the sin of slothfulness — and for the quagmire that pulls us, so subtly, in that direction.

Let us pray. God of the very best work ethic, we acknowledge that we like to paddle our own canoes. Sometimes we steer ourselves into the quagmire of life. Forgive us our "slack" and help us to get back on course.

Show us the benefit of a well-balanced life that gives attention to worship and study as well as to work and play. Help us to acknowledge, daily, that we give because we have received, generously, from Your bounty. Amen.

Thought for the day: Let us be diligent, watchful, lest we succumb to slothfulness and apathy — in our work habits, in our exercise regimen, and in our corporate and private worship of God.

Covetousness

Read Luke 12:13-21

Exodus 20:17: "You shall not covet...."

Someone figured out that more than a century ago the average person on this continent had 72 wants and sixteen necessities. Today, we have 480 wants and 93 necessities. Apparently we no longer know the difference between our wants and our needs. We see someone else with some new thing, and we immediately "need" it for ourselves — or for a family member. We will not be satisfied until the thing is in our possession. This excessive, unbridled desire for things has been identified as the classic sin of covetousness.

Covetousness bypasses the notion that we ought to learn to live simply so that others may simply live. It thrives on the compulsion to possess. If we see a golf buddy with the latest high-tech golf club which, supposedly, will improve our swing, we must have it, or we will be at a great disadvantage. A friend buys a new set of cookware, greatly improved over our current pots and pans, and we are green with envy. The next thing we know we are saddled with yet another "easy payment plan." We want/need a state-of-the-art kitchen and accessories while our skill is in choosing a good restaurant for family and friends to share with us in the breaking of bread.

Now the sin of covetousness might be more subtle than we staff members care to acknowledge. For example, are we secretly envious of the church member who drives the BMW? Who lives in the $750,000 home? Who has the wonderful cottage at the beach?

And what about our covetousness in this work place? We might not openly admit it, but might we be dissatisfied with the allocation of office space? In the purchase of new computers, were we overlooked, thus finding ourselves stuck with the older, slower models — or, heaven forbid, an outmoded electric typewriter?

Richard Foster, a Quaker philosopher and theologian, writes, "Contemporary culture is plagued by the passion to possess ... Obviously, there is nothing wrong with having things; it is the inordinate desire, the inner compulsion, the undisciplined craving that is condemned. Covetousness is the idolatrous worship of things."[1]

According to Foster, Americans comprise six percent of the world's population, yet we consume 33 percent of the world's resources. If the rest of the world were to attempt to live at our level of consumption, it is projected that all the known resources of petroleum, tin, zinc, natural gas, lead, copper, tungsten, gold, and mercury would be exhausted in ten years. Simply speaking, the earth cannot afford the American lifestyle.[2]

In our lifestyle, we are reluctant to admit that we often love things and use people. Yet in our reflections upon the Christian life we *know*, full well, that the opposite is what is intended. Even staff members get caught in this web, and Jesus' words ring as true as they did in New Testament times, "Take heed, and beware of all covetousness, for a man's life does not consist in the abundance of his possessions" (Luke 12:15). Perhaps our devotion ought to be a stewardship one. If we are not into the spiritual discipline of tithing, maybe we should, at least, experiment with it. Tithing might be our best safeguard against the sin of covetousness.

Let us pray. O God, Provider of a multitude of blessings, forgive the private boundaries we draw around the accounting of our stewardship. We make little or no distinction between the things we want and the things we really need. We believe that whatever we earn is ours to do with as we please.

Yet we are workers in your vineyard. We need to give a good account of our stewardship. We need to be pacesetters in this area of life. Aid us in lessening our inclination to accumulate things. Amen.

Thought for the day: Covetousness completely bypasses the notion that we ought to learn to live simply so others may simply live.

---

1. Richard J. Foster, *Freedom Of Simplicity* (San Francisco: Harper & Row Publishers, 1981), pp. 1, 18.

2. *Ibid.*, p. 127.

Gluttony

Read 1 Corinthians 10:23-24, 27, 30-31

Proverbs 23:1-2: "When you sit to dinner ... note well what is before you and put a knife to your throat if you are given to gluttony."

When I was growing up, there was in the capital city of our state an "S & W Cafeteria" where my father always wanted to eat whenever the family went there for whatever reason. He laughingly referred to this establishment as the "See & Want Cafeteria." That is the tag I have put on gluttony and lust; they are the "see and want" sins that get our physical natures into big trouble.

Gluttony is an inordinate yearning associated with our sense of taste. Most people want to think of it simply as a matter of overeating. For Americans, that is its most common form — but it is a more subtle sin than just stuffing our stomachs with food.

Like all sins, gluttony is the perversion of something that is good and right. Food and drink are absolute necessities for bodily life. Because they are necessities, they naturally offer a strong attraction. This classical sin enters in when a person responds excessively to this craving. In the thirteenth century, for example, Thomas Aquinas expanded the definition of gluttony, saying first that it consisted in eating and drinking too much. He then added that it was a matter of eating and drinking too fast, too often, too greedily, too expensively. Such acts, Aquinas said, had no patience to wait, no self-discipline (restraint).[1]

Today people are weight-conscious, calorie-conscious, fat grams-conscious. Some are absolutely exercise freaks. If we pick up almost any magazine, we likely find articles on how to lose weight. If we turn on the television, we are likely to find exercise programs, especially in the mornings. Yet studies show that the vast majority of us who lose weight, through carefully designed diet and exercise programs, usually gain it all back. It is just a matter of time.

105

Again, gluttony is not simply a matter of stuffing ourselves with food. Many can curb what they eat but cannot control what they drink. When I was a teenager, I learned an old adage which says, "First, a man takes a drink; then the drink takes a drink; then the drink takes the man." For the adage to be absolutely true, gluttonous drink can lead to alcoholism — and, most certainly, to periodic episodes of drunkenness.

Pressures at work and/or strains in their family relationships cause some persons to seek relief/escape through drinking alcoholic beverages — or by using other drugs in an abusive fashion. Such persons may, at least, become problem drinkers, whether they choose to admit it or not.

And if gluttony is defined as intemperate desire, then the case must be made about excessive smoking, or coffee drinking, or soft drinks, or chocolate intake — anything — which is potentially injurious to our health.

Not only for the reason of the potential endangerment to our physical well-being, the sin of gluttony can also dull our eyes and close up our hearts to the plight of other people. Consuming most anything, excessively, other than water, is expensive and selfish. It kills our sense of compassion and makes mockery of our profession that we love our neighbors as we do ourselves (see Matthew 19:19).

Paul wrote this very key thought when the issue of gluttony was brought to his attention, "And everyone who competes for the prize is temperate in all things" (1 Corinthians 9:25).

Let us pray. Sustainer God, we live in a land "flowing with milk and honey," as the Promised Land was so aptly described. Food and drink have been plentifully and attractively available to us. Consequently, we are encouraged toward excessive consumption.

Help us to see, clearly, the benefit of moderation in all things that are permissible and/or good for us. Let us not be found with a hole in our hearts because we have spent our money, wastefully, on our selfish desires. Give us the resolve to stick to good health habits. Amen.

Thought for the day: If gluttony is defined as intemperate desire, then the case must be made about excessive smoking, or coffee drinking, or soft drinks, or chocolate intake — anything which is potentially injurious to our health.

———————

1. The Reverend Dr. Joseph B. Mullins, *PEAS Can Grow Larger: A Contemporary Guide to the Seven Deadly Sins*, published by First Presbyterian Church, 617 N. Elm St., Greensboro, North Carolina, p. 30.

Lust

Read Matthew 5:27-28; 1 Corinthians 6:18-20

Matthew 5:28: "... anyone who looks at a woman lustfully has already committed adultery."

Galatians 5:19: "The acts of the sinful nature are obvious: sexual immorality, impurity, and debauchery."

Lust is the second of the "see and want" sins. It may be defined as wholly selfish sexual desire, with a double and triple emphasis on "selfish." On the one hand, *eros* love (sexual love) is a good gift from God within the context of Christian marriage. On the other hand, we sometimes degenerate that expression of love and may refer to it as "X-rated." Such expressions of love can be absolutely disgusting until we are in their grip; then they can be powerfully attractive. Lust is out-of-bounds and can only lead to disappointment and hurt. The fall-out of such behavior can affect many persons — and our local church — before it is all over.

A long time ago, the word "lust" stood for excessive desire of any kind: for food, drink, money, power, or pleasure. This is the way the word is used in the old King James Version of the Bible. Today, however, the word is used almost exclusively in the sense of selfish sexual desire. And it is still fairly common to use the word in conjunction with power-hungry individuals.

Can lust be a problem for church staffs? We all know of instances where it has been. Things begin innocently enough in the work place, but momentum builds. Soon, a relationship, or an action, has gone too far.

Lust always can be traced back to poor choices and decisions which appeared to be harmless at the time they were initiated. We do not fall in a moment when we are on this kind of journey. The predisposition to yield to lust has been forming, building, germinating, bubbling — but not necessarily consciously so. Lustful acts have both a cumulative and a domino effect. Satan plants subtle stimuli, often subliminal ones. Then when our defenses are down, he influences an attitude or a small action. And when Satan has won a "minor" victory, he picks up the tempo. Soon the situation is totally out of control, and the "big fall," the "in chains" habit, has resulted.

Maybe it was a short visit to a porn site on the Internet — or a flirtatious comment in a chat room. Maybe it was a discreet visit to an adult bookstore. Maybe it was at a time when things were not going well at home, and we took a fellow staffer into our confidence. We were vulnerable. Maybe it was not a fellow staff member at all; maybe it was a church member.

Adultery and fornication ought to be in every Christian's vocabulary but in no Christian's practice. Those are tough teachings, we say. Some persons feel they are old-fashioned and out-dated. But who gives anyone the right to alter the teachings of the Bible? The authority of Scripture is a standard to which staff members must adhere.

Each person's struggle for purity is fought and won — or lost — in the mind. Plainly and simply, we are what we think about. Our character is dyed the color of our thoughts. If we give attention to garbage, if we continuously seek out people and places that encourage our lustful nature, then we are courting big-time trouble. As someone has phrased it, "I can't keep the birds from flying over my head, but I can keep them from building nests in my hair."

We would do well to remember that our physical bodies are temples for the Holy Spirit. We are, therefore, to honor God with our bodies (see 1 Corinthians 6:19-20).

Let us pray. In the design of things, O God, you gave us the gift of our sexuality. Forgive us and restore us quickly when we fall into immorality or impurity in the expression of our sexuality. Call to our remembrance that our bodies are dwelling places for your Holy Spirit. Help us to honor you in all that we do. Amen.

Thought for the day: Our character is dyed the color of our thoughts. If we continuously seek out people and places that encourage our lustful nature, then we are courting big-time trouble.

Part Seven

Staff Talks For Special Seasons And Days Of The Year

Advent — Christmas

Read Luke 2:4-7

1 Kings 18:27: "... Perhaps he is deep in thought, or busy, or traveling...."

The above quote from 1 Kings 18 is completely out of context; nonetheless, it does describe a lot of us during this Advent season — and it connects to a feature article on Mrs. Lillie Swindell, a resident of Kitty Hawk, North Carolina, at the time of Wilbur and Orville Wright's first successful airplane flight. The brothers launched their flight from a sand dune, no more than a stone's throw from where Mrs. Swindell was living. She could have seen history in the making, if she had bothered to look out her window that day in 1906. Thinking that they were like children playing with kites, Mrs. Swindell was inside her house and did not bother to look out. "I didn't know what had happened until it was over,"[1] she stated.

Is that not a resemblance to what happened in Bethlehem long years ago? Mary and Joseph had come to this little town, as had many others, for the express purpose of the enrollment for Caesar's taxes. No one seemed to give a hoot for any other purposes, except that the innkeeper's wife possibly showed some small kindness to the woman who was so near her time to deliver. Folks were locked into their own thoughts, busy capitalizing on the enrollment, or, perhaps, wearied from traveling a distance for that purpose.

So the townspeople and the visitors to Bethlehem were no more than a stone's throw from history unfolding in their very midst. God was drawing near. Incarnate theology was being hammered out. The Word was being made flesh, so that God could live among us and experience all that we experience. A plan for our salvation was being launched. A road was being opened to eternity. Real estate was being made available — in heaven — at no cost to us.

If the people in Bethlehem had taken a careful look, they might have seen the glow from the cattle cave where, undoubtedly, Joseph had lit a fire to provide warmth for his beloved Mary and the

113

soon-to-be-born Jesus. When the birth was accomplished, no word was passed from house to house that a Savior was born that night and laid in a manger from which the livestock ate their hay.

A whole village, tired from the day's activities, nestled down to sleep, early. There was no television to watch, and no telephone or e-mail to pass along the gossip of the day. So they slept right through the most important birth in all of human history.

And when they woke up, they went right back to housekeeping responsibilities, or to plowing ground, or to minding their shops, or to their buying — and their enrolling for the great taxation — as though Christmas never really happened. Christmas was right there at their fingertips, and they missed it. Will we?

Will we be so preoccupied with our thoughts that we are insensitive to the needs of others? Will we be so busy that our busyness becomes the focus, and we miss the quiet, mysterious moment when Jesus could have been reborn into our hearts and homes — and into the hearts and homes of those whom we love and serve? Will we be so caught up in travel plans, of thoughts of visiting with our children, parents or grandparents, that we cannot sense that the distance between heaven and earth is shrinking?

Let us pray. Slow us down, Lord. Help us look for the guiding star and listen for the angel's song. Let Christmas put joy in our hearts again.

Forgive us that we insist on overburdened schedules and cluttered lives. Touch us in a new and wonderful way with comfort and peace from heavenly places. Do not let us miss the recall and the actualization of the greatest birth in human history because we think Christmas is only for children. Remind us that, regardless of our chronological age, we are — always — your children. Amen.

Thought for the day: At Christmas, God is drawing near. Real estate is being made available — in heaven — at no cost to us.

---

1. John Butler Justice, feature article on Mrs. Lillie Swindell, age 98, *News & Observer*, Raleigh, North Carolina, 1978.

Christmas
(The Great Efforts Of Christmas)

Read Romans 8:18-30; John 16:20-22

Romans 8:22: "We know that the whole creation has been groaning ... right up to the present time."

"Effort" means "the use of energy to produce something." That is the way it was that first Christmas in Bethlehem long years ago. God put a lot of himself into that Holy Event, knowing that it was into a sometimes cruel, cold, and unwelcoming world that he allowed his Son to enter. God needed no crystal ball to foresee that stones and insults would be hurled at Jesus in his adult life. God's vision was far-sighted enough that he saw the cross looming ahead. God knew the agony and the suffering that Jesus would face.

Yet God forged ahead with His plan to accomplish the holy birth. God's Spirit impregnated Mary. Overtime went into the effort to ensure that all the Old Testament prophecies concerning the birth would be fulfilled. Angels had to be instructed on how to carry out God's work — on earth as it is in heaven. Shepherds and wise men had to be inspired and motivated to respond in certain ways. God made good effort when he imagined that first Christmas.

And we do not need to minimize the effort of Joseph. He loved and trusted Mary, that she had, in fact, remained a virgin. Yet how could this thing be? She insisted that she was bearing God's child! So Joseph took Mary with him to Bethlehem, away from the gossip and scorn of Nazareth. The trip would have been no problem for Joseph traveling alone, but with Mary along, and in her condition, it was an arduous trek.

Once there, did Joseph serve as the mid-wife in delivering the Baby? Afterwards, as predetermined, he would raise the boy as his own. He would see to it that Jesus was loved by his siblings and accepted in the community where the family would live. It took great effort and determination on Joseph's part. Would you and I have done it under similar circumstances, if God had tapped us out from all other men, or if His angel had come to us in a dream?

Likewise, Mary put forth great effort. The cave, where the innkeeper directed Mary and Joseph, certainly did not have all the conveniences of home. Still, Mary made the best of the situation. She did not complain, as you and I might do if clean towels were not available and the covers were not turned back on a freshly made bed. She did not make life miserable, as we might, if the heating, air-conditioning, and color television (with cable) were not all in good working condition. And there was the smell of the animals, and the faint, if not prominent, stench of their wastes.

The only halo around Mary's head that night was a halo of sweat drops as she labored to give birth. And the straw, not the most comfortable thing upon which to lie, was stained with blood from her effort. John's Gospel indicates that Jesus as an adult had appreciation for his mother's effort — and for the effort of all mothers — in giving birth: "A woman giving birth to a child has pain because her time has come, but when her baby is born, she forgets the anguish because of her joy that a child is born into the world" (John 16:21).

December (Advent) is one of the busiest times of the year for the church staff. We possibly complain about all the efforts that have to be made, but when the Day has come and gone, may we remember only the joy that has come because the Holy Child, once again, has been born into our hearts.

Let us pray. Father of Jesus, we make our preparations each Advent-Christmas season because we think they are expected. You send the Gift of your Son in spite of our exerted effort. Jesus is born into hearts that are open to receive him, not into hearts that are too wearied to care. When the truth of his coming is revealed, may we feel extraordinarily blessed, and may our hearts be filled with joy. Amen.

Thought for the day: Like God, Joseph, and Mary, we, too, make our efforts but not always without complaint. When the Day has passed, may we remember only the joy that has come because the Holy Child, once again, has been born into our hearts.

New Year

Ezekiel 36:26: "I will give you a new heart and put a new spirit in you...."

A number of years ago, a cartoon depicted a school-aged boy standing before a stationery counter in a bookstore. He was asking the clerk, "Do you have any blank report cards?" A lot of people, reflecting back, can identify with the predicament of this youngster.

Fortunately, good grades are not required to get us into the kingdom of God. There is nothing we can do to earn a place in God's house. Yet the doors will be opened wide to receive us. Any staff member should be far along in understanding God's grace and how the gift of salvation applies to the individual's life.

Nonetheless, the idea of new beginnings should be exciting and challenging. The days of a new year are blank, waiting to be lived to the fullest and best that we can achieve with the help of Christ in the inner person. The possibilities are unlimited. In how many of the days will we make earnest application to the things of God?

What follows are ten resolutions that the staff might find helpful as they share together in ministry to God's people:

1. Resolve to be a little more patient with each other as we go about our work and as our lives touch with the sheep (church members) of this pasture (local church);

2. Resolve to be a little less prideful because of all we know in our area of expertise and a little more open to the suggestions of others;

3. Resolve to maintain our dignity and worth, while recognizing the dignity and worth of others;

4. Resolve to be a little more forgiving and swifter to be kind;

5. Resolve to utter, sincerely, words of encouragement and praise to others;

6. Resolve to listen compassionately to the hurt of others;

7. Resolve to seek a more positive attitude for an unpleasant task that, nonetheless, needs to be done;

8. Resolve to be a better team player in the staff lineup;

9. Resolve to let our little light shine as brightly for Christ as possible;

10. Resolve to seek first God's kingdom, and his righteousness, in each new day (see Matthew 6:33).

Let us pray. Kind and loving Father, we thank you that you have ordered life in such a way that new beginnings and new opportunities are frequently available to us. Give us the thrill of venturing forth. Make us strong in our desire to seek and to do your perfect will. Amen.

Thought for the day: The days of a new year are blank, waiting to be lived to the fullest and best that we can achieve with the help of Christ in the inner person.

Suggestions: Discuss, briefly, the resolutions that are set forth. Would they be good ones for your church staff to keep? Would you change the wording of any of them? Are there any that you would add?

Epiphany

Read Ephesians 2:11-20; Matthew 5:14-16

Ephesians 5:14: "Wake up, O sleeper, rise from the dead, and Christ shall give you light."

A staffer once wrote in the church newsletter, reporting a train and school bus collision. Seven children were killed. Later, an investigation was launched. The signal man at the crossing was severely cross-examined. Nonetheless, he stood his ground, insisting that he was swinging his lantern vigorously. The next day a friend complimented him for holding up well under the barrage of questions and for sticking to his story. The signal man replied, "I was afraid the lawyer was going to ask me if the lantern was lit."

That story ties nicely into the story about a little girl who returned home from church one Sunday. She had heard a sermon on "Let Your Light Shine." She asked her mother what the sermon meant, and the mother explained that the light shone when we were sweet and kind and considerate of others.

The next Sunday in the kindergarten class the little girl caused such an uproar that the teacher had to have someone fetch her mother so that she might bring her daughter under control. The mother asked her child why she was behaving so poorly. Remembering the sermon she had heard the previous Sunday, the little girl blurted out, "I have blowed myself out."

Epiphany is a continuing celebration that light has come into the world in Jesus Christ. It is a remembrance of the wisemen from a far country who visited the cattle cave in Bethlehem and who honored the Baby Jesus with gifts of gold, frankincense, and myrrh. Gentiles (including you and me), previously excluded from "the covenants of the promise, without hope and without God," were being "brought near through the blood of Christ" (see Ephesians 2:12-13).

Amazingly, Epiphany has to do not only with Jesus' mission but also with our commissioning to do likewise. Like him, we are

119

called to preach peace to those who are far away and peace to those who are near. "For through him we both [Jews and Gentiles, church members and outsiders] have access to the Father by one Spirit" (see Ephesians 2:17-18). We can go through the motions of religion — church membership, buildings, equipment, programs, pledging a budget — but if the lanterns are not lit for the world to see, some poor souls are going to have a deadly collision at our crossing with the world and its culture. If we in the church have blown ourselves out, and there is no light — only darkness and confusion, hopelessness, and the presence of sin — then the consequences are more far-reaching than we have dared to realize.

A long time ago, there was a church whose light bill was only sixty cents a month. The light bill, possibly, spoke volumes about the church's life and ministry. Most likely, it was a church of little activity — of little spiritual energy. Its light seldom shone in the darkness of that community and in that small area of God's spacious world.

How are our lights right now — both as individual staff members and in the corporate life of this church where we serve? Unlighted? Blown out? Low voltage? Shining brightly?

For earth and heaven's sake, we have a mission to go and tell — and to invite people to come and see! "Awake, O sleeper, rise from the dead, and Christ shall give you light."

Let us pray. Redeemer God and Source of Light, we want to be candles lit by Jesus who seeks to bring comfort and cheer to a darkened world. Forgive us when the light has been inadequately attended to in our life and in the life of this church.

Excite us to possibilities to be involved in missions. Keep us open to those outside the faith who are representative of the Gentiles of our day, so that they may be brought near to Christ and included as members of your household. In the strong and wonderful name of Jesus, we pray. Amen.

Thought for the day: If the lanterns are not lit in our churches for the world to see, some poor souls are going to have a deadly collision at our crossing with the world and its culture.

Lent
(What Are We Doing
With The *Now* of Our Lives?)

Read 2 Corinthians 4:7-12, 10-18

2 Corinthians 4:16: "Therefore, we do not lose heart...."

This is the time of the year when we think of the cross and reconciling love. We think of homes and relationships that need to be strengthened. We think of our nation's problems and the world situation and wonder what the population would look like if we all lived under the banner of Jesus' love and kingship.

Interestingly, both hope and fear look toward tomorrow. Fear causes us to dread tomorrow because we are afraid that life will only be worse than what we experienced today or yesterday. Hope, on the other hand, embraces tomorrow, eagerly anticipating all that a new 24-hours will bring. Hopeful people forget yesterday's mistakes fairly easily, affirming that yesterday is for learning and not for punishing. Better still, Christian people look toward Easter and resurrection and for the upward swing of life!

Second Corinthians 4:7-10 is a tremendous affirmation of the Christian's faith: "We are hard pressed on every side, but not crushed; perplexed, but not in despair; persecuted, but not abandoned; struck down, but not destroyed. We always carry around in our body the death of Jesus, so that his life may be revealed in our mortal body." Then verse 16 makes this powerful statement: "Therefore, we do not lose heart. Though outwardly we are wasting away, yet inwardly we are being renewed day by day."

This passage says we *all* suffer in life. There are setbacks and mishaps, trials and tribulations. There are thorns and thistles which produce prickly pain and sharp pain. But there are also forward strides, good gifts, tender love, sacred memories, and beautiful roses among those thorns and thistles.

So much is dependent upon our attitude and ability to handle the *now* of life. We must see the broad spectrum of life, the sum of our days — and not the divisibility of heartaches and disappointments. When laid end-to-end, life is good, and blessings abound. However, when we take the dim and narrow view, life hardly seems worth the living, and the work of the cross is negated.

John Jakes wrote eight novels which chronicled the place of the Kent family in our nation's history. The last in the series traces the life of Eleanor Kent, who, for so long a time, was not able to escape the horrors of her past. Her mind was tormented because she was "gang raped" as a teenager in her own home. Her marriage to Leon Goldman ended tragically because of the bigotry of a man who hated Jews. Because he died thinking all the problems in their relationship lay with him, Eleanor almost lost her sanity.

Later, she married Rafe Martin, having responded to the depth of his caring. She spoke of Rafe as "an incredibly kind man."

> *"The hell I am," he said. "I'm no saint. I'm just like ... one of those fellows who digs around old Arabian ruins and turns up a beautiful, old lamp worth millions. You don't find them throwing away such a treasure just because it has a few nicks and dents."* [1]

The best thing we have going for us in this life is that Jesus lived and died for our sins. Today can be well-lived because Jesus triumphed over the cross. The transcendent power belongs to God and not to us. The fact of our dents and scars pales in the light of his glory and grace.

Let us pray. God, sometimes we botch things up pretty good. Forgive us and love us in spite of the dents and scars, the blemishes and the shortcomings.

Jesus is the best thing we have going for us in this life. Help us to live *now* to the fullest and best that we know. Give us hope for all of our tomorrows. Amen.

Thought for the day: "But we have this treasure [Jesus] in jars of clay to show that all this surpassing power is from God" (2 Corinthians 4:7).

---

1. John Jakes, *The Americans* (Garden City, New York: Doubleday, 1980).

Maundy Thursday
(Last Meal)

Read 1 Corinthians 11:23-26; also Psalm 34:8

Mark 14:25: "... I will not drink again of the fruit of the vine until that day when I drink it anew in the kingdom of God."

Last meal? We do not want to think about *a final meal*. Our life centers too much on the *next* meal and what we might have as a snack before that time. Perish the thought of a last meal with a family member or the closest of friends!

Last meal? We would rather think of the last meal *we* ate. Was it lunch or supper? At home or in a restaurant? Was it short order, leisurely dining, take-out, international cuisine, or "down-home" cooking?

The mood and setting of Jesus' last meal with the twelve disciples is hard to grasp. It was Passover, and the meal was intended to be a celebration. Instead, it seems almost certain that the mood was somber. Jesus knew that his crucifixion was at hand. Tension was being felt. Something out-of-the-ordinary was about to take place.

The Apostle Paul wrote of the incident eighteen to twenty years later: "For I received from the Lord what I also passed on to you ..." (1 Corinthians 11:23). Obviously, Paul received his information from others who had been with Jesus. He himself was not yet a Christian on the occasion when Jesus instituted the Supper. History recalls this particular sharing of the Passover meal as the "Last Supper." Christians celebrate it as an ongoing Supper for those who wish to keep his commandment, to "do this in remembrance of me" (1 Corinthians 11:24).

In verse 24 Paul also recalled that when Jesus had taken the bread, he had broken it and given thanks. That was the Jewish practice. It should be the Christian's practice every day. Why not renew saying grace at meal times during this Lenten season if you have slipped away from the practice in recent weeks, months, or years?

A sibling of mine used to pray a rote blessing from her childhood without any real thought to what she was saying. She said, "O Lord, make us truly *and* thankful for what we are about to receive." I would smile and think to myself, "How can we be truly *and* thankful?"

We can, however, be truly — sincerely and earnestly — thankful for the broken body and the shed blood — and for the many other tokens of God's love for us. The Lord's Supper is life-giving nourishment for our souls. Daily bread is life-giving nourishment for our bodies. Thanks for the first should be greater than thanks for the latter, but both are imperative!

The "last" Supper anticipates the "next" meal of Holy Communion with the living Christ. And Jesus should be present at every table, including breakfast, lunch, and dinner.

Let us pray. Lord, make us truly thankful for the bread and wine. Meager, at first glance, these elements constitute the greatest Banquet we can eat in this mortal life. Amen.

Thought for the day: Saying grace, remembering to give thanks, ought to be the Christian's practice every day. And ... we ought to anticipate the "next" occasion when we can share at the Lord's Table.

Suggestion: The staff may choose to celebrate communion at the staff meeting. Before actually receiving the elements, let the members share that for which they are "truly thankful."

Easter
(A Follow Up To "Feed My Sheep")

Read John 21:15-19

Have you ever taken the time to study faces in a crowd? Perhaps it was on a busy city street or at a football game or even in church as people worship. There are laughing faces and sad faces, thin faces and plump faces, pretty faces and not-so-pretty faces, intense faces and relaxed faces. Perhaps the most revealing thing about a person's face is the eyes. Eyes express love, devotion, alarm, guilt, hate — a multitude of things.

Do you sense that Jesus was making a study of Peter's face as John's Gospel reports a third instance where the resurrected Jesus revealed himself to his disciples? Is it possible that Jesus might be reading our faces as we sit in this staff meeting on this day?

Simon Peter had thrice denied the Master on the night of his betrayal by Judas. The words Jesus now spoke to Peter took the form of a three-fold question and a triple commission, corresponding to Peter's triple denial. In actuality the three questions were really but one. Jesus studied the man's eyes intently. He saw there the emotion of love. He also saw the guilt and shame for not admitting his association with Jesus when put to the test. Now Jesus' probing questions and steady gaze only intensified the bad feelings.

But the questioning was also a catharsis. Before it was all over, Peter had emptied the heavy burden of his guilt and shame. Jesus had to know if Peter was ready for all that was to come. Would Peter always prove to be hot-headed as when he drew the sword and lopped off the servant's ear in the Garden (see John 18:10)? Or would his loyalty take a nose-dive when personal danger strongly surfaced and when popular opinion was running against the Jesus-movement? Would Peter prove to be incapable of handling the leadership role Jesus would give him? Jesus had to know, and it is with that same kind of searching and probing that he studies our faces and looks into our eyes as we are assembled as a church staff.

Peter wisely did not protest or argue when Jesus repeated the question, "Do you love me?" the second and third times. He was aware now that he was being challenged. There was little evidence of his steadfast devotion to put forward. Peter remembered the crowing of the rooster. Still he knew that in the far reaches of his heart he did love Jesus, in spite of everything to the contrary. So his reply was not intended to be argumentative. It was simply a statement of faith: "Lord, you know all things; surely you must know that I love you" (John 21:17).

Likewise, circumstances and times of denial cannot alter the fact that *we* really do love Jesus, down deep. Yet there is no denying that we fail him at times. We falter, we hesitate — and this makes any claim of our love seem ridiculous. And yet our affirmation of love is accepted by the living Christ. He is patient, faithful, merciful, forgiving, and understanding of us every day of our lives.

Jesus reminds staff members (disciples) that his call to a life of service must be repeated over and over again. Daily contact with the risen Lord is needed. If Jesus' call is heeded, he has but one commission, the same one he gave to Peter three times: "Feed my sheep!" (John 21:17).

Let us pray. Holy Father, we come before your presence affirming our loyalty and devotion. Yet, under close scrutiny, we do not measure up. Nonetheless, you instructed Jesus to say to us, "Take care of my sheep."

What that really means is that we are to think of others. We are to be a servant people. Cause us to see strong possibilities for ministry and outreach in the name of Jesus. Give us love strong enough and pure enough that others will know that our identity is with you and that our association with Jesus is undeniable. Amen.

Thought for the day: Jesus' call to discipleship must be repeated over and over again. If the call is heeded, there is but one commission: *"Feed my sheep."* Easter people, like Peter, you, and me, shake off our past and foster greater love among the flock.

Pentecost
(The Whole Purpose Of God)

Read Acts 2:1 (NKJV); Acts 20:25-31 (NIV)

Acts 20:28: "Keep watch over yourselves and over all the flock of which the Holy Spirit has made you overseers. Be shepherds of the church of God."

Pentecost, the church staff recognizes, is right up there in importance with Christmas, Good Friday, and Easter. Yet we never seem able to convince the congregation which we have been called to serve that this is the case. Pentecost, that day when the Holy Spirit came upon some really downcast disciples and transformed them into effective messengers of the Good News of Jesus' resurrection, calls us to search for the revitalization of Jesus' disciples in our day.

Now if we have served in this sheepfold long enough, we have shared with members of our church family the fullness of life — and sometimes the draining away of that life. We have watched some move from the fringes of our shared life to the forefront. Unfortunately, we have also witnessed the opposite: some who were quite actively involved have fallen away into inactivity. Sadder still is when no one seems to notice the drifting away.

In Paul's farewell speech to the elders of the church at Ephesus, there are a number of clues to resurrecting the important place of Pentecost. One is found in Acts 20:27 (TEV): "For I have not held back from announcing to you the whole purpose of God." Purpose has to do with the reason for the Church's being after nearly 2,000 years of existence. Why is a little brush fire that started long ago in Jerusalem still ablaze across the entire globe?

Verse 28 says, "Keep watch over ... *all* the flock...." The senior pastor may be the main shepherd of the flock, but the minister of music also has a responsibility for shepherding those under his or her care; likewise, the ministers(s) of children and youth.

128

This verse also reminds us of the most important person in the mix of the first Pentecost with Christian implications. It is the Holy Spirit who brought power to transform lives and who *calls* us to be overseers. We are to be channels of the Spirit's power, giving instruction and example on how to live, triumphantly, when the popular sway of life is toward secularism (see vv. 29-31).

Look back at verse 22 where Paul says, "And now, compelled by the Spirit, I am going to Jerusalem...." It seems, in our day, that we do not fully understand the Spirit's movement which is like the wind we cannot see and like the fire that purifies but does not destroy. We are not always obedient to the Spirit's leading, and we drain off his power by insisting that we will do things "our way." By contrast, when we initiate actions that grow out of his leading, we are being directed toward God's perfect will for our lives.

We resist praying to be filled with the Spirit — in each new day. To be filled with Jesus' Spirit has something to do with housecleaning and with breaking down walls of resistance. We should pray to be humbled and crushed as Christians until we are willing to clean out all that hinders the Spirit's space in the temple of our spiritual interior. His permanent residency in our hearts represents the whole purpose of God.

Has the day of Pentecost "fully come" for us? For this church (see Acts 2:1 NKJV)?

Let us pray. Almighty God, are we going to recall the history of Pentecost, or are we going to apply the lessons of Pentecost in our day and time? Without hesitancy on this day, we ask that You send your Spirit — with power, to fall upon us — and this church. Amen.

Thought for the day: Pentecost calls us to search for the revitalization of Jesus' disciples in our day.

Independence Day
(You Have Been Good To Us, Lord)

Read Psalm 119:43-48

Psalm 27:13: "I am still confident of this: I will see the goodness of the Lord in the land of the living."

When our family visited Philadelphia, we saw, among other things, the Liberty Bell and noted the inscription which reads: "Proclaim liberty throughout all the land, unto the inhabitants thereof" (Leviticus 25:10). Note, then, that the idea of liberty was not something newly discovered by our founding fathers. Liberty, as an intended blessing for all of humankind, has existed in the heart and mind of God for a long, long time.

As we approach July 4, thankfulness should come, not just for a day off and away from the church environs, but also out of our appreciation for God's place in our personal biography and in our nation's history. As Christians, we can ponder anew that he has redeemed us and freed us from the bondage of sin and death. And our gratitude should not overlook the fact that we dwell in a free land wherein God has allowed so many to live, to prosper, and to pursue happiness.

Our hearts should be stirred at the thoughts of Ben Franklin, John Adams, Thomas Jefferson, George Washington, and Valley Forge. And there have been countless others who wrote, spoke, persuaded, prayed, fought, and even died to keep this land free. It has never been easy — this thing called democracy. To preserve it has required the efforts of bluebloods, farmers, professional men and women, foreign-born and native-born, mountain men, cowboys, mill workers, housewives, pioneers, seamen, teachers, politicians, youth, common laborers, et al. The wars have seemed endless and cruel; the progress, at times, slow but steady.

Today there is a different feel to living as an American. No longer is our country a melting pot where people blend together as one people — a people showing allegiance to God and proper patriotism to nation. We are diverse — torn apart by varying opinions, by ideology, by irresponsible actions, by undisciplined and unrestrained behavior. There are senseless killings throughout the land, and acts of unbelievable violence occur in our schools. Child abuse is incredibly high. And there is a youth culture that is often selfish and out of control. Garbage, air pollution, and streams filled with sewage are a major concern.

As professed Christians are often biblically illiterate, so today's young Americans are showing incredible holes in their knowledge of our country's history. In a survey conducted by Caravan ORC International, 1,020 teenagers, representative of about 24 million U. S. students between ages twelve and seventeen, results showed that 22 percent did not know that the colonies declared their independence from Great Britain during the Revolutionary War; that seventeen percent did not know that there were thirteen original colonies; that fifteen percent did not know that the Continental Congress adopted the Declaration of Independence on July 4, 1776; and that ten percent did not know that George Washington was the country's first president.[1]

Are we not baffled today when the Fourth of July is observed as a day to bask in the sun, to watch fireworks, to enjoy a family, company, or church picnic, to drink lemonade, to have a pig-picking, and so on — and there is no recall by the young, middle-aged, or older citizenry of our nation's great heritage?

Yes, there is plenty that is wrong, but there is still more here to be thankful for than anywhere else in the world or at any other time in history. As the Psalmist said, "I am still confident that I will see the goodness of the Lord in the land of the living."

Let us pray. You have been good to us, Lord — beyond belief. We are privileged to live in a land flowing with milk and honey, with food and goods beyond measure. The beauty of the land that comprises these fifty states is absolutely awesome. Our freedom is truly remarkable.

Today we acknowledge that you are the source of every good and perfect gift. Help us to live responsibly before you and our neighbors and friends. Thank you for a marvelous heritage. Amen.

131

Thought for the day: Liberty, as an intended blessing for all of humankind, has existed in the heart and mind of God for a long, long time.

Suggestion for Discussion: How might we lead our church family to keep a more meaningful observance of July 4th?

---

1. *The Herald-Sun* newspaper, Durham, North Carolina, July 3, 2001, Section A (front page).

Thanksgiving

Psalm 95:2: "Let us come before him with thanksgiving...."

1 Thessalonians 5:18: "Give thanks in all circumstances...."

In a study made by the London *Times* many years ago, some British children were asked, "What are the twelve loveliest things that you know?" One child replied,

> *"The cold of ice cream, the scrunch of dry leaves, the feel of clean clothes, water running in a bath tub, climbing up a hill and looking down, cool wind on a hot day, honey in my mouth, the smell of a drug store, the feeling inside when you sing, babies smiling, and little kittens."*

That list conjures up pleasant memories even as we hear them recited.

For our staff talk this morning, I want to pass out a piece of paper and ask that you write twelve lovely things for which you are thankful. Do not include people. At the end of our devotional time, we will share some of the things on our list.

How quickly we forget the lovely and good things of life — and the news of good report! This is the danger of relegating thanksgiving to a day proclaimed by our President. To paraphrase an old popular song, "Thanksgiving knows no season; Thanksgiving knows no clime; Thanksgiving should blossom any old time."

God's benefits exceed our ability to enumerate. But to appreciate God's generosity, we must foster a personal relationship with him. Thanksgiving does not spring up like a root out of dry ground.

King Alfonso XII ruled over Spain many, many years ago. It came to his attention that pages in his court neglected to ask God's blessings on their daily meals. So he invited them to a banquet which they all attended. The table was spread with every kind of good thing, and the boys ate with apparent relish. But, as had been reported, not one of them remembered to express thanks to God for the abundance which was theirs to enjoy.

Suddenly, a beggar entered the banquet hall, dirty and raggedly clad. He seated himself at the royal table and ate and drank to his heart's content. At first, the pages were so taken aback with the man's poor manners that they said nothing. They expected that the king would order the beggar to be thrown out, but Alfonso never opened his mouth.

When the beggar had his fill, he rose and left without a word of thanks to his host. Then the young men could keep still no longer, "What a terrible fellow!" they cried. But the king silenced them and in a clear, calm voice said, "Boys, bolder and more audacious than this beggar have you all been. Every day you sit down to a table supplied by the bounty of your heavenly Father; yet you ask not his blessing, nor express to him your gratitude."

The farmer probably expresses thanks for the ingathering of his crops, but the Christian, according to the writer of 1 Thessalonians, is to "give thanks in all circumstances." In the dark hours of pain, sorrow, and grief, we may suppose our circumstances to be evil and certainly of no positive value. But God is at work in the midst of our troubles, seeking to bring comfort and to shed light on our path. Given time, perhaps years, God might transform our terrible heartbreaking experiences into blessings. A time of significant growth in our faith and character formation may be the lasting result toward which we are moving.

A medieval Jewish saint said, "I shall take the broken fragments of my heart, and of them I shall build for Thee, O God, an altar." The altar built by the Jewish saint was the altar of thanksgiving.

Let us pray. Kind and loving God, we realize that we have not been constant in expressing appreciation for the good and lovely things of life. These common, everyday blessings do not include the extraordinary things that are occurring in medical research and in other spheres of our existence. Help us, O God, to translate our thanksgiving over into thanks-living. Amen.

Thought for the day: Share, at least four or five things, from your list of the loveliest things for which you wish to give thanks on this day.

Suggestion: The leader should write out his or her list of twelve lovely things for which you are thankful in advance of the staff meeting.

Part Eight

VITs With The Church Staff
(Very Important Talks)

Faith

Read Matthew 8:23-27

Hebrews 11:1: "Now faith is being sure of what we hope for and certain of what we do not see."

Yesterday is for learning. Today is for living life to the fullest and best that we know. Tomorrow is for hoping that life will be better. That is a good philosophy for those who want to have a forward look to all their days and not be chained to the past and to failures and disillusionment.

As Christians, have we not wondered how people live life without faith? How they stretch their lives over a thin-threatened today? How they survive the onslaught of an unexpected crisis when there is no rope of faith to seize?

Imagine for a moment what our lives would be like if our faith in Christ suddenly vanished from plain view and comprehension. It would be like a marriage from which love has suddenly evaporated — only worse! It would be like the coldest night with no heat to provide us warmth — only worse! It would be like the sun burning out with no promise of daylight following darkness — only worse! It would be like a fog that never lifts — only worse!

As staff members, we have a strong commitment to nurture faith not only within ourselves but also in the church members who are the sheep of this pasture. Many churches today have family life centers; such facilities often house gymnasiums. We seek to minister to the whole person, and physical fitness is certainly important in that regard. Lately, I have been thinking that our churches need to be spiritual gymnasiums where our faith muscles are toned up and made to be game-ready for the world out there.

Jan Karon is a refreshing author who has written about Father Tim, a parish priest in a small-town setting. In the very first book of the Mitford series, she has Cynthia Goldsmith saying these words about Father Tim: "He sees to it that our faith gets pushed and pulled, stretched and pounded, taken to its limits so its limits can expand ... If it doesn't get exercised, it becomes like a weak muscle that fails us when we need it."[1]

It is not only the pastor who exercises our faith muscles and pushes them to new limits through his sermons and in the conduct of his life; it is every staff member in the pursuit of his or her daily responsibilities. The youth pastor does not plan a "lock-in" at the church for the sole purpose of another activity on the calendar or for the mere entertainment of youth. Somewhere in that activity there should be the notion that the faith muscles of the youth will be engaged in "spiritual calisthenics."

The minister of music and the organist do not challenge the choir to entertain or to perform great musical pieces, only because time is allotted for such purposes in a service of worship. Choir members are singing for the purpose of ushering the worshiper into the very presence of God. If a contribution is made in this regard, the exercise of faith expands us into wishing, at some future time, to be in the heavenly host that gladly sings the Lord's praises — daily!

If our God-consciousness has grown too dim, it is because our faith in God is not being massaged, exercised, toned up, challenged, nurtured! Right now, this very minute, we are on holy ground. God is Emmanuel — here with us! Let us celebrate his presence at our staff meeting!

Let us pray. Excite us, O God, about your Presence with us in this very room! You want us to know that you are closer than our breath.

Bring faith into sharper focus than ever before. If we do not exercise it from day to day, it becomes a lost treasure. Help us not to be lacking when the swells of life thunder down upon us. Hold us, O God, in the hollow of your hand and close to your heart. Amen.

Thought for the day: Our churches need to be spiritual gymnasiums where our faith muscles are toned up and made to be game ready for the world out there.

Suggestion: Discuss how it would be to discover that God is as near as our breath, even closer. Is our faith making us sense more and more that we are on holy ground? That we are in his presence, right now?

---

1. Jan Karon, *At Home In Mitford* (Elgin, Illinois: Lion Publishing Co.), p. 158.

Home And Family

Read Deuteronomy 11:18-21; 1 Timothy 3:4

1 Thessalonians 3:6b: "... He has told us that you always have pleasant memories of us...."

A friend wrote me a post card during his visit to Pennsylvania Dutch country. The card carried in "Dutch English" this message: "Too soon old; too late smart." It is a wise saying to apply to home life. Time flies swiftly by, and before we know it, our children have left home. The wisdom we had meant to impart, we feel, was never measured out in even doses. We only hope time will prove to be in our favor and that our offspring will lean more to the pluses of their upbringing and less to the minuses.

When Moses was giving instructions to the Israelite children on God's wishes, he knew, full well, the importance of building up memories. He reminded the people to: "Fix these words of mine in your hearts and minds; tie them as symbols on your hands and bind them on your foreheads. Teach them to your children, talking about them when you sit at home, and when you walk (ride) along the road ... Write them on the doorframes of your houses ..." (see Deuteronomy 11:18-20).

This may be one of the most important talks we can have together as a church staff. The pull of culture is strong against Christian nurture in the homes of our church members. There may be days and days when there seems to be no time to sit down together for a family meal. In the rush of things, the blessing of food is easily overlooked. To whatever degree people look to the staff for example, let us not be found lacking in our attention to home and family.

Balancing family and responsibilities at the church can be a difficult task, and the demands of our church family can easily eclipse the needs of our immediate family. Paul's instruction is that our first priority is to manage our own family well and see that our children obey with proper respect (see 1 Timothy 3:4).

Emily Ashton Tipton wrote that "home ... is where parents and memories live." A most important question for us to consider is this: "What will our children remember about home?" The following seem to be essential:

- that the Christian faith is being taught and practiced with consistency;
- that the evidence of love is so strong that it gives our children confidence for all their tomorrows;
- that forgiveness is readily applied to the irritations and blemishes of a young child's conduct;
- that the children have positive attitudes about their church home and about staff members, and especially the pastor;
- that they plainly see that their parents love each other;
- that there is familiarity with the practice of prayer in the home and that members are growing beyond rote prayers to being comfortable in praying spontaneously, thus strengthening a personal relationship with the living God;
- that each person in the home is cultivating the ability to laugh, not at the expense of someone else's feelings but with the good purpose that life is to be celebrated — every day!

In summary, each positive memory is a diamond; each negative memory is a rock. If our children collect enough rocks against home and family, their burden is heavy. Their memories ought to be mostly diamonds, and the love they receive from God and parents ought to be the most highly polished treasure they possess.

Let us pray. If our homes are not resting on the strongest foundation possible, Lord, give us the determination to make it a top priority. May we apply, generously, a spirit of kindness and understanding with all with whom we live. Forgive us when we have been too long on presenting our point of view and too short on listening to the point of view of those whom we say we love.

If our homes have not existed as fortresses sheltering hearts against a culture that appears to be out-of-control; primary schools that teach spiritual truth and right values and that mold character; miniature churches providing worship and settings for spiritual growth; give us grace and strength to change our living quarters toward a better end. Amen.

Thought for the day: Our children's memories ought to be mostly diamonds, and the love they receive from God and parents ought to be the most highly polished treasure they possess.

Vacations

Read Luke 5:15-16; Psalm 121:1-2; Psalm 51:10-12

Psalm 51:10: "... and renew a steadfast spirit within me."

Three men come to mind when I think of vacations: one was a farmer, the second a businessman, and the third a senior pastor. The farmer almost bragged to me that he never took a vacation. His work ethic was too strong — his responsibilities too many. The businessman, likewise, said he never took a vacation; yet he and his wife were constantly going on little business trips to interesting and exotic spots. They were season ticket holders to his college's football and basketball games and to any post season play in which the school was involved. My guess is that he was chintzy in offering his employees vacation days and that he held out to them that dedication to work — with little or no time away from the office — made him an envious success. Who did he think he was kidding?

The senior pastor claimed the full time the church allowed him for vacation and when he returned to work, there was every indication that the church would be the beneficiary of his rest and renewal. He hit the ground running, and the rest of the staff fed off his energy, ideas, and vision.

The point: I have never known a farmer, a businessman, an employee, a pastor, a staff member, a housewife, a student — anyone worth a grain of salt — who did not need a vacation. Vacation comes from the Latin word *vacatio*, which means being free from a duty, service, and so on. Quite literally, it means to vacate, to step away from one's routine responsibilities; to take time away from one's office and work.

The biblical record does not indicate that Jesus took vacation time once he began his three years of public ministry. By vacation here we mean days and weeks away from his work of teaching, preaching, and healing. But let us not be deceived. Luke 5:16 reveals that Jesus often withdrew to a lonely place and prayed. When

145

people demanded too much from him and when the crowd pressed too closely, Jesus had the disciples row their fishing boat far enough away from shore that he could gain perspective — through conversation with his heavenly Father. Or — he retreated to the mountains, there remembering the words of the Psalmist: "I lift up my eyes to the hills — where does my help come from? My help comes from the Lord, the Maker of heaven and earth." Jesus' "time off" may be viewed as mini-vacations, but they had maximum benefit.

This matter of vacations is a very important talk with staffers. Some suggestions and reminders might be in order:

1. Take a regular day off each week. This means five work days, not six, and most certainly, not seven. These mini-vacations will have maximum benefit in the performance of your responsibilities.

2. Remember to schedule longer vacations at least a month in advance. Do not "surprise" the senior pastor by being away from your post upon his return from his vacation. He may be counting upon your presence when he hits the ground running.

3. Emergency leave, or personal time off, is not the same thing as the aforementioned day off or extended vacation days. If your staff does not have firm policy on this issue, you might want to formulate one and pass it along to the appropriate church committee which has oversight over the staff for their approval/ adoption.

4. When you leave for vacation days, be certain that your desk is in order and that all ongoing responsibilities have been delegated or otherwise covered.

5. Do not return to work more tired than when you left. If your vacation has involved heavy travel, allow one day at home to rest up before returning to your responsibilities.

In summary, let us remember that Jesus retreated so that He might be renewed. We, too, need time apart, else we might come apart at our emotional seams.

Let us pray. God of the mountains and God of the seas, we thank you for the vastness of your world and for the places that beckon us to come and renew ourselves. Help us to use well our time apart.

Wherever we go and whatever we do, remind us that we are never away from your presence. Return us to our work place with our cup running over and not drained dry. Give us a willing spirit as we return to our servant roles. Amen.

Thought for the day: We need time apart (a vacation), else we might come apart at our emotional seams.

Urgency

Read Matthew 9:36-38; John 4:35-38

Matthew 4:35: "... open your eyes and look at the fields. They are ripe for harvest...."

The senior pastor, from the pulpit, was requesting that the congregation pray for the church's youth who had gone "out" into God's mission field for a week of work and witnessing. He wanted us to pray for their safety and for their effectiveness in their labor of love. The mission field, I thought to myself, is not "out there." It is in our homes, in our neighborhoods, in our rural areas, towns, and cities. It is not just two counties or two states over from where we live — and it is not identified only to be in Honduras, Cuba, Africa, China, or the former countries of the Soviet Union. No, the mission field is wherever people live, move, and have their being. Our mission is to everyone who has not been personally confronted with the life-changing gospel of Jesus and his love.

And there is an *urgency* about the delivery of that gospel that only intensified with each passing day. Jesus recognized it. He cited the familiar Jewish proverb about four more months of waiting for the harvest. Maybe four months represented the growing season in Israel. And the translation over into current Christian thought is that the seed of the gospel has been sown for nearly 2,000 years now. The Greek word "work" in John 4:38 earlier in the chapter has this application: tired or wearied (see John 4:6). Sowing, cultivating, and harvesting are arduous tasks, not only in the physical realm but also in the faith realm. People have been doing the first two of those tasks for a long time now, and it is no longer the seedtime or growing season that is in question. The fields are ripe unto the harvest. The work is difficult, but eternity hangs in the balance. Let us not be too lazy, or too tired, for the work of a harvester in the fields.

The late Bishop Kenneth Goodson, addressing an Evangelism Conference in Miami, Florida, said there is not much difference between seventeen and eighteen persons being saved, unless the eighteenth person happens to be your son or daughter. Then it makes all the difference in the world. Urgency suddenly becomes a major issue.

Too many young people today — our children and grandchildren — no, too many people today (all ages) are postponing a decision about taking Christ seriously. They nod in God's direction but do not take a step closer to him. Tomorrow — or the day after — will be soon enough, they reason. "You fool!" God said. "This very night your life will be demanded from you" (see Luke 12:20). Some may not like the urgent tone of those words, but it is better to live with the dislike than with the regret of its truth.

Dennis Rainey is a recognized author and worker with Campus Crusade's Family Ministry. From his pen came these words, "As a college student, I lived my life in two different spiritual conditions. For the first two years I was a mission field; the last two years I was a missionary."[1]

This is a very important talk together. Are we a mission field — or a missionary? And what of our children, other family members, friends, neighbors, and co-workers? Are we tools for their harvest into Christians? Are we faithful laborers in the vineyard, or have we wearied in well doing? "For at the proper time we will reap a harvest if we do not give up" (see Galatians 6:9).

Let us pray. Lord of the harvest, we want to be found faithful in our labors in your vineyard. Patience is a virtue, but urgency is a mandate. Do not let us miss an opportunity to speak a good word for Jesus. Eternity hangs in the balance. Amen.

Thought for the day: "You fool!" God said. "This very night your life will be demanded of you." Some may not like the urgent tone of those words, but it is better to live with the dislike than with the regret of its truth.

---

1. Dennis Rainey, *Pulling Weeds, Planting Seeds* (San Bernardino, California: Here's Life Publications, 1989), p. 1.

Motivation

Read 1 Chronicles 28:9-12

1 Chronicles 28:9: "... serve [God] with whole-hearted devotion and with a willing mind, for the Lord searches every heart and understands every motive behind the thought."

How many young people have been pushed by their parents into a debate about life's strongest motivator — love or money? Of course, there are other motivational factors. Young people and the young-at-heart are challenged by a dare. When we acquire wisdom and experience, we are less likely to be prompted to act foolishly on a dare.

An assistant coach at a major university was a member of our church in one parish setting. He served under two head coaches. When I asked him the difference in their styles of leadership, he thought only for a moment before responding. The first coach, he said, would cuss his players, belittle them in front of their teammates, get in their faces and yell at them. It was all external motivation. By contrast, the second coach praised his players for the things they did right. He built up their confidence. He set a fire burning within their hearts — genuine desire to play hard and to win, if possible, but to be gentlemen in losing. His motivation was internal, and when the players came onto the field to play a game, they were sky high with their enthusiasm. They were fun to watch — in victory or defeat.

In truth, a multitude of things motivates us: the influence of parents; praise; the intense desire to accomplish a goal; the profit motive; a thirst for knowledge; peer pressure; a good example; the promise of reward; the fear of punishment or failure; one's competitive nature; the wish to succeed; the press of time; the pursuit of a dream. If we made an exhaustive list of all the things that motivate us, we hope there would be more positive stimuli than negative ones.

When I was in divinity school, morning worship in the chapel was conducted by the seniors or, on occasion, by a faculty member. Only one sentence by an upperclassman has stuck in my thoughts for all these years. He said, "If the love of God doesn't move you, there's no need to scare the hell out of you." That is a strong thought to plant in the hearts and minds of any staff member who may be a part of this morning's devotional talk.

There is a wonderful Bible study concerning motivation in the book of 1 Chronicles, chapter 28. David is driven by the dream to build a magnificent temple for Jehovah God. He is thwarted in those plans by God himself (see v. 3). So he trusts his parental influence over Solomon and charges him with the task of bringing the dream into the realm of reality (vv. 9-10, 20). And before formally passing the dream along to his son, David uses his leadership and the promise of reward to solidify the dream in the hearts of the people. He says, "Be careful to follow all the commands of the Lord your God, that you may possess this good land and pass it on as an inheritance to your descendants forever" (v. 8).

Verse 9 is an extremely well-framed truth: "... for the Lord searches every heart and understands every motive." There is nothing we can hide from God. God understands the temptation to slack off from work and routine, and he knows the weight of our intention to serve him with our whole heart.

What is our motivation on this day? Are we working for a pay check or are we seeking his will for the way we are undertaking to get things done?

Let us pray. Father of infinite wisdom and great compassion, thank you for knowing us so well. You understand our moods and emotions and our reasons for doing things — and for not doing them. Challenge us to be faithful to you — not to be task driven or motivated by a need to be successful. Above all else, help us to be controlled by love in all that we think, say, and do. In his strong name we pray. Amen.

Thought for the day: "If the love of God doesn't move you, there's no need to scare the hell out of you." (Divinity school senior, 1958-59)

Vision

Read 1 Chronicles 22:1-19a

Proverbs 29:18 (KJV): "Where there is no vision, the people perish...."

In 1954, the Reverend Ralph Arthur was assigned to be President of Ferrum Junior College in the foothills of the Blue Ridge Mountains. His instructions were either to bury the institution or to resurrect it. Now Ralph Archer was a resurrection person with a vision. Never did he give even a moment's thought to burying that small, struggling college with its dilapidated buildings and an approximate enrollment of 100 students.

Four years later, C. P. Minnick, Jr., was sent to be the chaplain at Ferrum. President Archer stood on the steps of his home and readily shared with him his vision for the College, pointing out exact locations for eleven new projects, including a chapel and bell tower, dormitories for both male and female students, a student union building, and a library. Minnick reports that he stood quietly and listened and thought to himself, "This man is a foolish dreamer. Never will all this happen here...."

But it did! Twelve years later, Minnick returned to the College for the Memorial Service for President Archer who died at age 52 from cancer. But not before God used him mightily! In C. P. Minnick's own words, "I stood there and looked all around me. There it was, all in place, just as he had dreamed ... There were more than 1,200 students enrolled ... And all of this had happened because one man had a vision and refused to let go until it became a reality...."[1]

The story of President Ralph Archer gives credence to the Old Testament proverb, "Where there is no vision, the people perish." The truth can be extended to the death of a college, a nation, a business, and yes, to a home and to a church.

Among my favorite lines of poetry are these:

Dreams are they — but they are God's dreams.
Shall we decry them and scorn them?
— That men shall love one another ...
— That greed shall pass from the market place ...
— That men shall meet with God face-to-face.
Dreams are they all, But shall we despise them —
God's dreams?[2]

Within this church where we work as a staff, there is a faith story that speaks of vision and sacrifice. Some, if not all the buildings, were built against tremendous odds. The reality of the dream did not happen overnight. It took a few people who gained a vision — who shared God's dream — that a church building needed to be erected on a certain plot of land. Because they dreamed in concert with God's dream, those buildings stand today, a symbol of the unity and strength of God's people.

But the dream is never ever just for the physical properties and accessories. We do not need an edifice complex. The dream includes persons being engaged in meaningful worship and being personally confronted with the living Christ; people of all ages growing in the faith, knowledge. and love of this Christ, and their burdens being lifted and their heartaches being healed; and this church family having a mission outreach that keeps going and going like Duracell batteries.

King David was not allowed to build a house for the Lord "because you have shed much blood on the earth in My sight ..." (1 Chronicles 22:8b). Yet it was in David's mind and heart that the idea was conceived. Verse 1 of chapter 22 has David saying these words: "The house of the Lord God is to be here...." The dream never dies, only the dreamer. Solomon, David's son, brought the dream into technicolor reality.

No one needs to take the credit for the dream that is waiting to be played out in this church. It is God's dream (see 1 Corinthians 3:5-9), and without it, the church will perish. Generalities in the dream are fairly common in every vital, growing congregation. However, the specifics are quite different. We are God's fellow workers and his field for cultivation (see 1 Corinthians 3:9). Plainly

153

and simply, let us check to see if our dream is in complete harmony with God's plan.

Let us pray. Master Architect, imagining God, your mind is too great for us to absorb all of your ideas and dreams at once. So you give it to us in small — and, at times, in sweeping — pieces. We are enthralled whenever you reveal it to us.

Today we want to check in and see if we are in agreement with where you are seeking to lead us in this church. As a staff we have a tremendous responsibility to make sure our church family life is dreaming in concert with your vision. Give us unity and strength in our undertakings, and may Christ be glorified in all that we do. In his strong name, we pray. Amen.

Thought for the day: "Our dreams at times will become as flat tires on our cars. But at other times, our dreams will lift us, like the second stage of a rocket, closer to the truth of God." (Emil Paul John, Providence, Rhode Island)

Discussion: Are we being obedient to the vision (see Acts 26:19) for this church? Where is he taking us?

---

1. Bishop C. P. Minnick, Jr., Presiding Bishop of the North Carolina Conference of the United Methodist Church, sent me a detailed copy of his recollection of President Ralph Archer's vision in October 1993.

2. Thomas Curtis Clarke, "God's Dreams," 1917.